MMXI

THE WHITE REVIEW

EDITORS	BENJAMIN EASTHAM & JACQUES TESTARD
DESIGN, ART DIRECTION	RAY O'MEARA
EDITORIAL ASSISTANT	ISABEL BLAKE
CONTRIBUTING EDITORS	JACOB BROMBERG, J.S. TENNANT
SALES AND DISTRIBUTION	COSIMA HIBBERT
READERS	JONATHAN BERRY, RAHUL BERY
TRUSTEES	MICHAEL AMHERST, HANNAH BARRY, ANN & MICHAEL CAESAR, BLAINE COOK, HUGUES DE DIVONNE, TOM MORRISON-BELL, NIALL HOBHOUSE, AMY POLLNER, PROFESSOR ANDREW PEACOCK, CÉCILE DE ROCHEQUAIRIE, HUBERT TESTARD, MICHEL TESTARD, DANIELA & RON WILLSON, CAROLINE YOUNGER
HONORARY TRUSTEES	DEBORAH COX, WILLIAM MORGAN

COVER BY LEWIS IRVINE

PRINTED BY PUSH, LONDON
PAPER BY FENNER PAPER (STARFINE IVORY 100GSM, NATURAL WHITE 115GSM)
BESPOKE PAPER MARBLE BY PAYHEMBURY MARBLE PAPERS
TYPESET IN JOYOUS (BLANCHE)

PUBLISHED BY THE WHITE REVIEW, JUNE 2011
EDITION OF 1,000
ISBN No. 978-0-9568001-1-4

COPYRIGHT © THE WHITE REVIEW AND INDIVIDUAL CONTRIBUTORS, 2011.
ALL RIGHTS RESERVED. NO REPRODUCTION, COPY OR TRANSMISSION,
IN WHOLE OR IN PART, MAY BE MADE WITHOUT WRITTEN PERMISSION.

THE WHITE REVIEW, 1 KNIGHTSBRIDGE GREEN, LONDON SW1X 7QA
WWW.THEWHITEREVIEW.ORG

CONTENTS

p. i   EDITORIAL

p. 1   THE SURREALIST SECTION OF
THE HARRY RANSOM CENTRE
by DIEGO TRELLES PAZ tr. JANET HENDRICKSON (F)

p. 9   GAY MADONNAS IN MONTEVERGINE:
THE FEAST OF MAMMA SCHIAVONA
by ANNABEL HOWARD (R)

p. 21   WILLIAM BOYD Interview

p. 41   SRI LANKAN CONTEMPORARY ART
by JOSEPHINE BREESE (A)

p. 51   PORTRAITS OF PIERRE REVERDY
AND THREE OF HIS POEMS
tr. SAM GORDON (P)

p. 63   THE END OF FRANCOPHONIE:
THE POLITICS OF FRENCH LITERATURE
by LAUREN ELKIN (R)

p. 75   FROM BACK HOME
by JH ENGSTRÖM (A)

p. 103   RICHARD WENTWORTH Interview

p. 113   CONFLICTS OF INTEREST: FRANK O'HARA
AND THE COLLABORATIVE TALENT
by THIRZA WAKEFIELD (E)

CONTENTS

p. 121   CAFÉDÄMMERUNG
and NOTES TOWARD THE CRANE POEM
by JOSHUA COHEN (F)

p. 147   I CLING TO VIRTUE
by NOAM TORAN, ONKAR KULAR and KEITH R. JONES (A)

p. 159   POETRY by GRAHAM FOUST, PATRICK MCGUINNESS, KIT BUCHAN, LEE ROURKE and AHREN WARNER (P)

p. 169   MICHAEL HARDT Interview

p. 183   RELIGION AND THE MOVIES
by AIDAN COTTRELL BOYCE (F)

p. 189   THREE POETS AND THE WORLD
by CALEB KLACES (E)

p. 199   APPENDIX

Cover:
Vy∃x (Rxy^¬Rxx)
by LEWIS IRVINE (typeset with RAY O'MEARA)

Poster insert:
DESTINATION UNPARADISE & ELUSIVE KNOWN
by SOPHIE VON CUNDALE (A)

PAGE INDEX:
{ A—Art, F—Fiction, E—Essay, P—Poetry, R—Reportage }

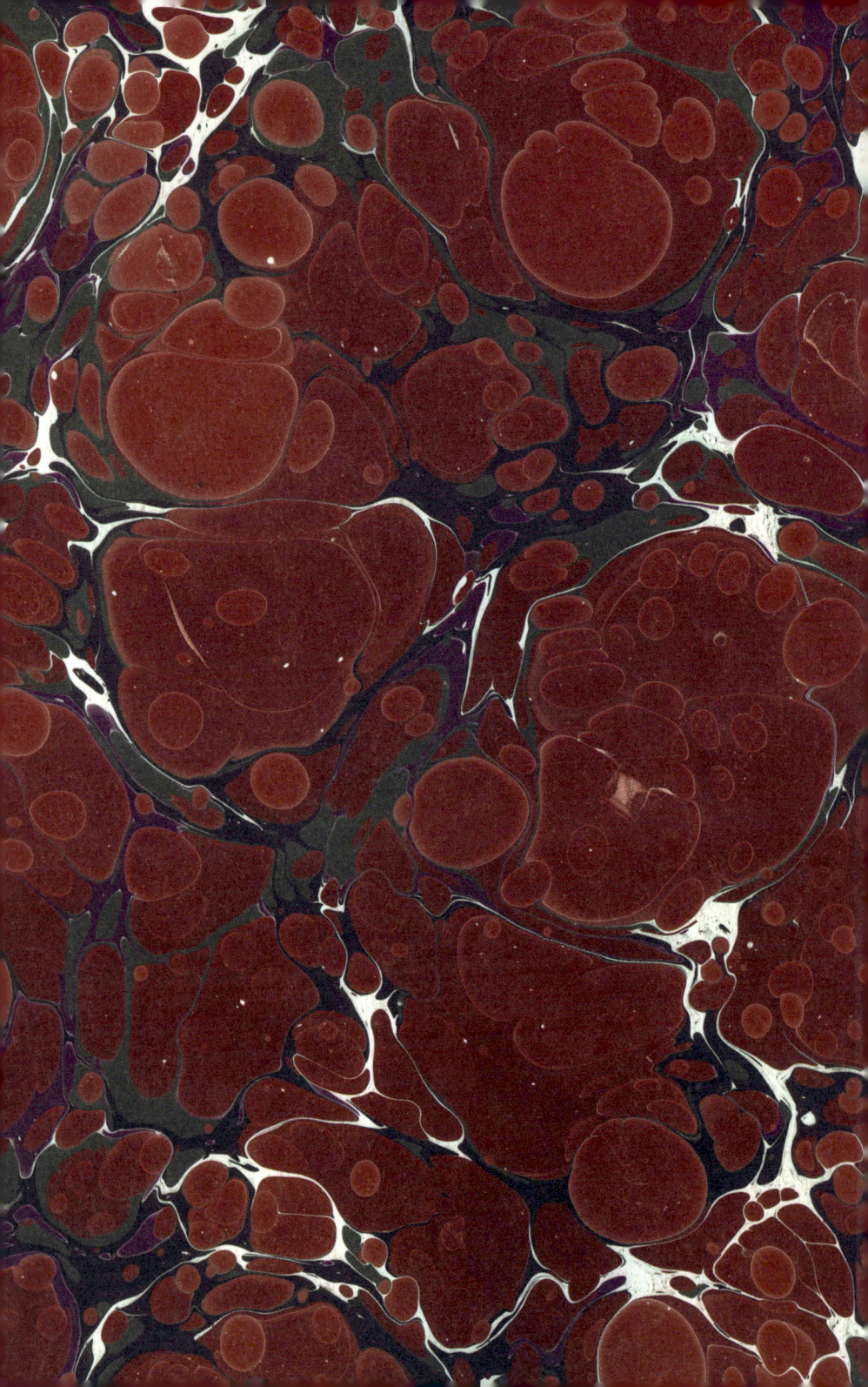

EDITORIAL

THERE HAS BEEN MUCH TALK IN THE MEDIA AND AROUND DINNER TABLES THAT PRINT IS DEAD OR DYING. THE WHITE REVIEW WAS FOUNDED IN PERHAPS FOOLISH DEFIANCE OF SUCH RECEIVED WISDOM. The reception of the first issue – which has enabled the production of a second – suggests that there is still some life in the medium. That there is space for a publication striving to bring together different forms and genres is reassuring to anyone with any stake – emotional or otherwise – in the potential for a renewal of the print tradition, and particularly the journal form.

It is perhaps too easy for writers and editors of our generation to leaf reverently through archive copies of *The Yellow Book*, *Blast* or *Horizon*, or to look back with a borrowed nostalgia to the 'glory days' of independent publishing – epitomised by the likes of Faber & Faber, New Directions or Olympia Press – and lament the market-driven conservatism of our own age. But the conservatism of the market is no reflection on the readership: new writers continue to emerge, and we hope to bring them to readers ill-served by a risk-averse publishing industry.

By allowing us to publish their work, the writers and artists featured here are helping to build a journal that will endeavour to stay close to new writing and emerging art in years to come. We are not yet in a position to pay contributors (or ourselves for that matter), though it is a priority for us to reward their creativity as soon as we are financially able. In any case, we are indebted to them for submitting their work without remuneration. We hope that the context in which it is reproduced justifies, for now, the time devoted to their art.

We try to resist the urge to impose a theme on each issue. Nonetheless connections emerge, organically, in the compilation of the journal. This second issue has poetry at its heart. We hope you enjoy it.

THE EDITORS

THE SURREALIST SECTION OF THE HARRY RANSOM CENTRE

BY

DIEGO TRELLES PAZ

(*tr.* JANET HENDRICKSON)

To Enrique Fierro and Ida Vitale —

JUST LIKE YOU, MUCHACHOS, I DIDN'T BELIEVE IN GHOSTS, and if I'd heard then one of the stories I tell Mario now, I would have said *poor guy*, and then I would have added, fully convinced, *he's crazy*, or maybe, *he's pretending to be crazy* or *he's lost it*, or better yet, *he's loco*, and the world, muchachos, listen up, this world is an endless black joke, but at least I – I don't know about you – but I, officer Warren Sutpen, ex-nightwatchman of the glorious Harry Ransom Centre of the University of Texas, here, at my forty-some years and ready to respond to the call, still find myself saved.

Saved from who or what? I don't really get it. I don't get it now, and I didn't before. And the thing is, before, say, a shitload of years ago, I didn't talk like this. For example, not six months ago, the word 'joke' meant something funny to me, like 'just kidding', or 'playing a trick', and 'black', I mean, 'negro', was just a little word I couldn't use, no, never ever, not to talk about los pinches negros, for instance. (Mario, my psychologist, calls them 'African-Americans', and if they're Chinese, they're 'Asian-Americans', and if they're Latinos, he calls them 'Hispanics' and if they're Hindus he calls them 'Indians', and so all this networking or whatever it is seems to go really well for him, since he says everything in this nice, musical way that I just can't imitate whenever he corrects me with his perfect accent and the manners of the white Texan he actually isn't.)

He also says two marvellous things about ghosts. The first: Warren – he looks at me, I listen – is that they seem very real, but really, they're the product of delirium, of a mental anomaly that's perfectly controllable if only you accept it, and of course, Mario, I accept it, and moreover, I've made that very clear to all the fucking ghosts. The second is that talking with them shouldn't be considered psychotic behaviour, as there are a number of occult sciences not entirely removed from the topic. Of course, this calms me down. I haven't felt calm since they fired me from the museum. Sometimes I'm overwhelmed by panic attacks. Sometimes I cry for a long time, until I fall asleep. On the days that neither of those things happens, I have a sick desire to put on my blue uniform and go back to the Harry Ransom Centre to wake up André and Antonin and Louis and Paul.

If it weren't for my poor old lady, who suffers more than anyone when I tell her these things, I would have done it already. I say old lady and I'm sure you think I'm talking about my mother, but you're wrong. My old lady, mi vieja, is my wife, Leonora Eulalia Campos Santos, the mother of mi guacho, the great Miguelito Thomas Sutpen Campos. This is my family and I am Warren Sutpen and I declare myself indebted, heart, body, and soul, to them and Trilce, our beautiful Lab, a German Shepherd Miguelito calls Spooky with an obstinacy he'll have to let go of when he wants to get ahead in life. Of course, the worst thing is that when I'm not there, Leonora calls him Spooky because according to her, Trilce isn't a healthy name for a pet. Mi pobre vieja. She doesn't even know what it means y ya está chingando. I've told her a thousand times that Spooky is a name for gringo dogs and faggot dogs and our dog is bien mexicano and if they hadn't cut his balls off, they would have been as big as a bull's.

Of course, it wasn't my idea to name the dog Trilce because I don't know what the fuck that means either, and I'm never one to make things difficult. It was the Peruvian's idea. My friend, el pinche motherfucking peruano who brought me all this bad luck. It goes more or less like this, Mario: the pig comes up to me one day and asks me about the dog, and I say, are you referring to Spooky? and he asks me what colour Spooky is and before I can answer he says that if he's black, Warren, black like death, you can't call the dog Spooky. Ah qué peruano matarife, I think, he ought to be a warlock. Spooky is black like Cujo from the movie. The Peruvian laughs and orders me (it felt like a friendly order) to honour Miguelito's brave Afghan with the name Trilce, and when I ask him why, he talks about the great César Vallejo and I imagine a red-skinned Indian just like the ones we exterminated a shitload of years ago in this pinche, hateful country.

But I'm wrong, of course: the great César isn't Indian and he doesn't have little streaks of blood on his cheekbones. He was a poor gentleman poet who wrote a very cultured book that no one understands. I'm telling you it's cultured, right? and the crazy asshole tells me it's *painful*, Warren, looking at me like he were constipated, as if reading made him feel like he were being punched. The day he shows up, I wake up early, kiss Miguelito on the forehead, and after eating the egg and chorizo tacos that mi vieja makes, I set off for the bus with my lunchbox. My regular days are this: bed–kiss–bus–museum, and on the way back, museum–bus–kiss–bed. I'm happy. Leonora's happy. Miguelito's happy. What else do we need to be happy? Not much. On the weekends we go to the movies or throw back a few pork tacos and a giant pozole at Arandas, or we go to the lake and cook up a barbecue listening to Los Tigres del Norte. At night, if my old lady's up for it, when Miguelito's already asleep, we close the door and I lie on top of her carefully and close my eyes, and for a little while my Leonora turns into one of those chavitas who clean the museum on the night shift. Of course, Leonora doesn't like it that I work at night, she's not an idiot. You already know, Mario, in spite of everything, I look white as bread, and I only speak English on the job, and that alone conjures up the girls who only have to see a friendly gringo to start dreaming of the green card I'd be happy to give them for just one pinche kiss. I'm telling you all this and repeating it to myself, knowing I'll never do anything because I'm just a poor pendejo.

So I'm telling you only what's happening now, not before, since before I was happy, Leonora was happy, Miguelito was happy, and there was nothing complicated in going from the house to the museum and from the museum home. But then, the stupid motherfucker pinche hocicón de mierda comes, and he plants himself right in front of me as if I owed him money. 'Sir, you know who the Sutpens were, correct?' el peruano says in Spanish, as if he were testing me. 'You're referring to my family?' I answer, pissed, putting the holster of my 45mm in my hands without any subtlety. 'The Sutpens are a family, yes,' he adds suddenly, looking at the ceiling with the air of an absent-minded philosopher, and I'm about to put an ugly end to all this bullshit when I hear what he asks me: 'Thomas Sutpen, is he a relative of yours?' Ah no, chingados, I tell myself, this asshole knows me, and so without thinking, I answer he's my father, and for a second, Mario, no, for five seconds, I see the old bastard sprawled on the porch of my house in El Paso, totally drunk, vomit all over his clothes, his face dirty with grease, and my mother asking me, Warren, take your father to his room, he's sick, and I pick him up and he tells me from the ground, 'tú no me toques, puto,' except in English, 'Warren, you nasty son of a bitch, you're a disgrace! Do you hear me? Don't you dare lay your hands on me, you faggot!' He laughed and I knew, Mario, that he was angry because my friends were from the border: Mexicans like me, even though I was a gringo, and Thomas Sutpen, my father, pointed all his rage at them and their fathers and their fathers' fathers and all of Mexico.

'Thomas Sutpen exists,' the Peruvian then says, smiling, and I know nothing except that now I feel a sick desire to punch him. I don't do it. In fact, I do the complete opposite: I sit down, fold my hands and listen to him carefully. 'Please don't let this bother you: the other day I came to the museum, and while you watched my backpack, I saw your last name on your uniform and remembered.' I didn't say anything. 'Sutpen, you understand? General Thomas Sutpen arrives in Mississippi after the Civil War and establishes a condemned dynasty, an incestuous, bastard breed, half white and half black. Do you know what I'm talking about? *Absalom, Absalom!* Sir, your father... Your father has the name of one of Faulkner's characters, and I've discovered it.' What a fucking moron. Just look at the asshole, coming up to me with his stories of miserable people and upsetting my life with his little coincidences that aren't worth dick. That's exactly when everything ends, Mario. The night falls suddenly, and I don't notice anything until the cocksucker comes back, smiling, with the novel, apparently to lend it to me. And what does the idiot Warren do? Nothing, he does nothing, he says, 'Thanks, I'll read it,' and instead of shutting his trap, he begins to tell the Peruvian about his son of a motherfucker father who must have died in the street because he hasn't heard anything from him for a shitload of years.

And then what, muchachos. Well, guess. Warren opens Mr Faulkner's book and reads and reads and spends two whole nights reading in the museum as if he were possessed. My old lady doesn't understand what's going on. Miguelito doesn't give a shit, he stays glued to the TV like an idiot. I tell Leonora I'm informing myself about our ancestors, and I also talk to her about our bloody origins, and for the first time in our fifteen years of marriage, I call my father by his name, and she looks at me with the eyes of someone who's suddenly grown afraid. Mi pobre vieja, she doesn't understand a thing. She wants to read the novel, but she doesn't know English, and every time I tell her about General Sutpen and how his sons kill each other because of an incestuous love that they know nothing about, she starts to babble something about the devil and the Virgin of God Knows Where and she bursts out crying and begs me on her knees to go to church, Warren, to pray for your soul. And of course, Mario, I go with her and kneel and make the sign of the cross and do everything just like Leonora, but like hell I pray, because I can't.

From then on, the days seem different, the bus rides are longer and more tedious, people stare at me, and I can't think straight in the fucking Texas heat. You know what I do? I don't only read all of Mr Faulkner's novels, but I go to the library like I were hungry for more. *The Sound and the Fury, As I Lay Dying, Sanctuary, Light in August*, all of them, I read all of them, looking for more clues, and the pinche Peruvian doesn't show up, not even by accident. One day, when I'm convinced that I'd just imagined everything, I see his fucking smile in front of my face and hear his voice saying, 'Warren, did you like the book?' and though once again I'm about to kick the shit out of him, I answer yes. From this day on we are friends, he says, and I say nothing. I don't have the guts to kick him out of the museum. It gets worse when he asks me about Harry Ransom's poets, and right then I realise that for the past three years Warren Sutpen has been the nightwatchman of a museum he's never seen.

That's what I'm thinking about when suddenly, for no reason at all, the Peruvian starts with the stories of these dead people. 'The Surrealists,' he says, with a mysterious passion, and I automatically think of those Mexican corrido bands I like so much. But no. I'm wrong, Mario. What the hell are the Surrealists? I don't know, I never understood. The Peruvian says they're here, in the Harry Ransom, as if they were sleeping on the second floor. My silence eggs him on, and so he starts bringing me books of strange poems that he leaves on the table. I read them at night, searching for more clues, but now I don't understand anything worth shit, and for the first time I feel the pinche Peruvian is leading me on. I don't say anything. I keep reading from inertia, I think. One night I get home from work, and when I try to sleep, Mario, something very strange happens: I can't. I have a shitload of words turning over in my head. Words that sound like women's and children's voices in unison. Words that make a sentence that says nothing, but I know I've heard it before. 'It's like a nightmare, but I'm awake,' I tell Leonora in the morning, and without holding back her tears, she immediately places a rosary in my hands and starts to pray.

Then she begs me desperately to stop reading. She tells me that reading is blasphemy and it only causes pain. She asks me to do it for Miguelito, and I tell her, 'Mi vieja, don't you worry about you and Miguelito,' although I would swear el cabrón de Miguelito doesn't notice a thing and keeps sitting like an idiot in front of the TV. That night, after all the museum employees have left, I keep looking at the pile of books and discover, to my surprise, that there's a new one. NADJA is the title and the author is André Breton, and I remember vividly that this pendejo is one of the dead poets that the Peruvian talked about. I imagine, then, that it's another indecipherable book, but upon opening it, I come across a story like Mr Faulkner's, except this time with photos and little drawings, and, hungry again, I devour the little book impatiently, looking for more clues. Nadja is a slippery woman, and she seems crazy. She's poor, beautiful, she prostitutes herself, and the narrator wants to save her. That's what I understand. But Mario, what suddenly makes me want to stand up aren't the strange noises beginning to echo through the museum, but rather, the underlined sentence that appears at the end of the text:

'Beauty will be convulsive, or it won't be.'

I can't believe it. It hits me: that was the phrase that the voices repeated in my sleep, Mario! I know it then, and at that same moment, when I stumble into the main room, I see the four of them standing, staring straight at me with the same damn smile I had already seen on the Peruvian. André and Louis and Paul and Antonin. The dead poets. They introduce themselves delicately. I approach them, unafraid, and we talk and talk and talk, and that's all we do until dawn. You already know the rest. I know what you're going to tell me now because you've already told me before. I've seen that security video several times and I understand the shirtless man who talks and gestures at the museum walls is me.

I've told hardly anyone what the ghosts told me. Once I told my poor old lady, and she fell into a swoon that I didn't think would end. It more or less goes like this: the day I leave the hospital, I pick up the phone and call my brother the puto (because I have a brother who really is a faggot) and after telling him a few lies, I get a few vague indications of the place where I can find him. I take mi vieja's truck and tell Miguelito that we're going for a ride. When Miguelito asks me if it's going to take long, I don't say anything; the place is an hour away, near San Antonio, and I know Miguelito is going to fall asleep on top of the dog in less than five minutes.

When I put my hand over mi pobre guacho's drooling mouth, Thomas Sutpen is less than twenty yards from us, with a cardboard sign in his lap, moving on his wheelchair between the cars. Miguelito asks me if we're there yet, and I tell him yes and silently show him this sick man begging on the roadside. I take a wad of bills out of my pocket and put it in Miguelito's hand. 'Give it to him and come back. Take Trilce with you,' I say, and mi guacho agrees. It's then, muchachos, just when I see mi guachito walking toward the old man, that I understand everything that's happened to me, and I know I'm saved. I don't care if Thomas Sutpen drinks up all the money in a day. I don't care that my son is giving my money to his grandfather without either of them knowing it. When Miguelito returns and asks why I'm crying, I tell him I don't know and try to smile, without any luck.

I'd like to watch TV with you, Warren Sutpen says, before starting the car and heading back.

GAY MADONNAS IN MONTEVERGINE: THE FEAST OF MAMMA SCHIAVONA

BY

ANNABEL HOWARD

WE ARE CROWDED INTO THE MEDIUM-SIZED PIAZZA before the sanctuary of Montevergine. There is no town or village; it sits alone near the top of an isolated mountain. A narrow road leads up to the sanctuary walls, which rise seamlessly from the sheer limestone incline. The buildings are simple: just a few square blocks tucked behind a rectangular bell tower and a tall, narrow church. They are uniformly pale, and at this time of year, in bitter winter, sit like dirty butter pats under a dusting of snow. The snow also covers the barren scrub of one of Italy's wildest regions, Basilicata, which unfurls with dreary panache in the valley one thousand metres below.

I am early and the cold drains the blood from my hands, rushes it into my cheeks and to the end of my nose. I'm even early enough to catch a candle seller so old that she seems to be made of stone. She is tiny and she sits against the wall. She is rotund only because she is wrapped in so many layers of blanket. What appears to be a blue pillow is tied to her head. She clutches her brightly-painted candles as though she doesn't really want to sell them, as though she'd rather donate them all to the Madonna that everyone is here to worship. When she realises that my real purpose is not to buy them, but to talk to her, she refuses to utter another word and looks angrily at the ground.

The old woman is selling candles because today is Candlemas. This is the official end of Christmas and the day on which candles are blessed in Christian churches all over the world. Candlemas is the oldest Marian ritual and one of the earliest to appear in the written sources.[1]

¶ Despite its imposing history, this celebration does not appear to be an entirely serious event. All over the piazza small groups are arriving. Most of them come from Naples, which lies sixty kilometres to the east of Montevergine. A lot of people carry unrecognisable instruments; many of them shake cymbals at the cold mountains. In the evening a mass will be held, and the blanket blackness of the church will be illuminated by the candles of the faithful. But for the moment prayer seems far from peoples minds: many of them are singing, and even at this early hour, some have begun to drink and dance.

Almost everyone is wearing a long thick quilted jacket – shades of black interspersed with provocative orange, olive and purple. A modicum of glamour resides in the synched-in waists and the faux-fur trims which float around Michelin-man hoods. Only the older members of the crowd are dressed demurely in heavy felt, black and white scarves tied around their heads.

Everyone is moving except Angelo, who is rooted, solid as a rock, in their midst. His curved body is topped by a black flat-cap on grey curls, and he is so short and

---

1. There are several vague references to a sermon on the subject of Candlemas, given by the Bishop of Patara, on the west coast of Turkey in 312, before Christianity was even legalised. A more reliable source was the intrepid nun Egeria who, during her three-year pilgrimage to the Holy Land (381-384), wrote a full account of the service (see Gingras, G., Egeria: *DIARY OF A PILGRIMAGE*, 1970, The Newman).

round it is difficult to tell whether he is sitting or standing. He has a blooming jowl, deep-set eyes, and resembles nothing so much as a very amenable scone. He is here to sing popular Neapolitan songs. He holds an instrument which is like a great wooden fork with movable prongs. The prongs are straight, square, and very blue. When he shakes himself about they clack together like giant castanets. I ask him what the instrument is called, but he seems to think it is needless curiosity to give it a name:

'Oh, this in my hand?' he says, and looks down at it as if he's never seen it before: 'How would I know? It's in my hand, I play it.'

Many groups are singing and playing, but for the whole motley chorus the performance is a sideshow: everyone is waiting for the Mass. And the star of the show is the Madonna, the Madonna of Montevergine, whose stately procession is winding its way up the hill. Over the course of the year a constant stream of pilgrims come to see her, and about two thousand of them arrive on this day, 2 February.

There are literally thousands of Madonnas in Italy; what makes this one so special? For it is not just the likes of Angelo who are here, nor is it your average church crowd: pilgrims of all shapes and sizes spill from the bright red cable car that's transported them the last 300 metres up the mountain. The steep road is becoming choked with buses that glint aggressively in the harsh light. They trail out of the tiny parking space and breathlessly wheeze open and wheeze shut their doors. From one a flock of laughing, flirtatious, outrageously dressed figures flood onto the snow. There is something unsettling about them – most of them are women and they are either mannered or mask-like under their heavy make-up, all red lips and chunky blonde hair. It's hard to lay my finger on what exactly is out of place. They bring a buzz as they flow raucously into the crowd clotting at the bottom of the steps leading to the church.

¶ The crowds come because this is *their* Madonna, the Madonna of the people. There are many earthy locals here to worship their Virgin protectoress in strange little songs which praise her for being the one person capable of loosening the bonds of life. The crowd, glamorous blondes included, adore this Virgin, who they affectionately term 'Mamma Schiavona' (or Slave Mama), because she is ugly, and because she is black. She, not unlike them, drew the short straw, yet still managed to end up as the Queen of Heaven.

Mamma Schiavona not only provides a precious ray of hope, but also has some important practical jobs to perform. She heals illness and finds husbands for unmarried girls. Rather idiosyncratically, it is she who helps her devotees to win the lottery. The proceeds of this talent are, I am unsurprised to note, not much in evidence at the festival – the attendants are decidedly shabby.

I contemplate the likelihood that, in a similar environment, I would also pray fervently for a stake in my rather precarious future. While I mull over my answer I stare blurrily through my thought at a lady mincing along in front of me. And suddenly I am aware that she's *actually mincing*, twirling her bare torso and pink feather boa on theatrical tiptoes, periscoping sideways over thrust-out shoulders, under spinning castanets. And of course I realise what was so odd about all those women: they were not women at all, this is not a woman, and nor is 'her' partner, who now I realise is enormous, and has a jaw of steel and a greasy low ponytail. Not even their retinue: one broad-shouldered, well-wrapped figure, slowly flipping a cymbal which flashes in the sun. Or am I imagining things now? No, he's bending towards me and blowing a kiss from thin scarlet lips that glow from behind a slight darkening of stubble.

This, then, must be where the edge comes from, the hum through the crowd, the schoolboy sense of transgression: a significant fraction of the crowd is gay or transgender. And that, in an Italian Catholic environment, is more of a shock than the freezing mountain air. What *are* they doing here, in the bosom of the notoriously homophobic Catholic Church? The answer meanders through history and in doing so takes in an ancient earth-mother cult, Renaissance Neapolitan rent boys, and the extraordinary culture of acceptance that exists in this corner of Southern Italy.

¶ These men (for they are uniformly men) are known as *femminielli*, and they have made the journey from Naples, where they live and work. *Femminiello* literally means 'little-man-woman', but a more accurate English translation would probably be 'rent boy'. The *femminiello* is not actually transsexual. He dresses as a woman but for most observant passers-by he is recognisably male beneath his feminine façade. He makes his living through prostitution.

Femminielli were first recorded in Naples during the sixteenth century. By this point in its history the city had been submerged under the waves of greater European forces for centuries. Naples, beautiful and rich, a key strategic port for both defence and trade, has always been worth fighting over. Its history reads like a rather poetic shorthand of the struggle for power in Europe – rulers of Naples: Greeks, Romans, Byzantine Emperors, Lombard Princes, Normans, Hohenstaufen, Anjou, Aragonese, Spanish Hapsburg, Bourbon…

In 1502 it was the Spanish who marched into the city. They set about the issue of control with a heavy hand. They garrisoned a whole platoon of troops in an area of Naples that is still known as the Spanish Quarter. It is a sizeable chunk of the city, and its plan retains a military grid to this day. The logical form of the grid was meant to provide a network of streets that would facilitate Spanish control over the unruly population. It's ironic that such a chaotic city had some of the earliest and most logical urban planning in Europe, all of which is still visible, neat and ordered, on the Neapolitan town map. It is even more ironic that it was the Spanish soldiers themselves who brought, along with discipline and parallel streets, an impetus for the underground world which consequently bloomed, quickly embracing the new market for prostitutes of both sexes who happily made themselves at home in this old–new section of the city. Indeed the prostitutes became an accepted part of society, and when the Spanish left in 1714, they overran the Spanish Quarter, where to this day chaotic lawlessness paints itself around the right–angled, neat streets.

¶ Walking around Naples today, it is clear that everyone knows everyone else's business. Knowing others people's business is a fact, no, a *prerogative* of Neapolitan life. You cannot cover twenty metres without seeing an old man sitting on a bollard and quietly dry shaving as the crowd bashes past him; or witness a voluptuous young girl suggestively eating an ice–cream in front of not one, but a crowd of young admirers. In Northern Europe it feels voyeuristic to glance through a street window and glimpse supper being prepared, or a flash of somebody else's television. It is impossible to take this attitude in Naples; if you did, you'd soon feel the need to blindfold yourself, for the people might as well not build walls to their homes. Through gaping great windows and wide open doors you see whole families sitting in front of a blaring TV in cheap, ground floor, single–room apartments; seven or eight people are squashed onto a sofa–bed, stuffed between a sink, a hob, and the battered communal scooter. The volume is loud enough that at the far end of the street the background game–show jingle still quavers with speaker static. Even this is sometimes drowned out by a cross–street conversation, which may be about something as mundane as what good fish there may be for sale in the market that day. To an unfamiliar ear, it sounds like a heated argument. Worse though, is when the family silently stare, not at the TV screen, but out into the street, and meet a curious gaze with a mixture of resignation and melancholy.

In this environment the *femminielli* used to flourish. The Neapolitans loved them and still do. They quickly became a part of the street furniture in the poorer quarters of the city. When the Spanish eventually ate up their own power in the Wars of the Spanish Succession and were forced to leave Naples, the *femminielli* had their heyday. They became firmly established and by the eighteenth century Naples had become one of the sexual capitals of Europe, drawing visitors from all corners of the globe, later famously hosting ex–inmate Oscar Wilde.

The *femminielli* colonised the Spanish Quarter, but despite laws against prostitution, and despite the homophobia and prudishness of the nineteenth century, they were never exorcised from society. In fact, they were and are accepted and adored. Why? Because the *femminiello* is an integral part of Naples' social fabric. In the past he was often a younger son in a large and poor family. The child's good looks provided a relief for the family, who would have pushed him towards his future in order not only to relieve their financial situation, but also to considerably supplement it. Nowadays the family pressure is largely removed, but the reward is the same and just as tempting – a successful *femminiello* can make a considerable amount of money through prostitution.

The *femminiello* 'chooses' his calling at an early age, and pursues it with the vigour of an apprenticeship. He learns to dress, to sew and to crochet with the local women. He learns to flirt and to apply his peculiar make-up. Most importantly, he learns to be a semi-permanent performer, an entertainer, almost a clown. This is important because he is the street mascot; the person that your baby must be photographed with the moment it is born; the person that you desperately want to draw your lottery numbers; the person who entertains and enlivens the community. In return he is awarded a strange social liberty and becomes a star player in the microcosmic environs of the street.

¶ The *femminielli* do not trek for sixty kilometres into the hills just because the Madonna is a protector of minorities. They come because Montevergine is the site of an ancient pagan cult. This was not any old cult, but the spot where the goddess Cybele had her temple. There was not much rational about Cybele, who was a hang-over from the great early civilisation mother-goddess cults, which died out in Western Europe with the Phoenicians in about 3000 BCE. Cybele, however, lived on through the cultures of Greece and Rome. She was the mother of all the gods, associated fundamentally with the earth, caves, and wild nature. Her cult was Eastern, and probably has its roots in the Bronze Age. Representations of her dating back to the sixth century BCE litter the Middle East, from ancient Anatolia right across to Afghanistan. Her devotees celebrated her cult with night-long orgiastic ceremonies, in which explosive drumming, drunkenness and torch-lit dancing were essential elements. This ritual was transferred to Rome where it was described by the poet Catullus:

> the clash of cymbals ring, tambourines resound, the Phrygian flute-player blows deeply on his curved reed, and ivy-crowned maenads toss their heads wildly.

According to myth, Cybele was in love with a young man named Attis. Attis, however, fell in love with and married another woman. In a fit of rage Cybele cursed him so that in a state of ecstasy he castrated himself and bled to death in front of his wife and the goddess. Cybele was deeply remorseful and, full of regret, brought Attis back to life, ensuring his chaste devotion by recreating him in the form of a fir tree. Cybele's exclusively male priests developed their identity under the influence of this myth. They not only removed themselves from the sexual game by assuming a role in which they were neither man nor woman – growing their hair long and dressing in female clothing and jewellery – but many of them also physically precluded themselves from any sexual activity by a dramatic ritual self-castration.

¶ Pagan cults in Italy were viciously stamped out in the fourth century, yet the temple at Montevergine survived long after Constantine legalised Christianity in 313 CE. The temple even survived the retributive destruction that spread through the newly Christianised world under the Emperor Theodosius I. Between 379 and 395 he issued a series of decrees which made any public expression of the ancient pagan cults illegal, and any practice of them, or implicit support of them, punishable by death. Despite this Cybele's followers at Montevergine practised their extreme rituals right into the eleventh century.

How did the Montevergine temple and its following survive? This is a bit of a mystery, and one which is not made any clearer by the murky mixture of unreliable sources which chart its history. The most likely (and most mundane) explanation is that its remoteness, and the devoted – but most importantly contained – zeal that it incited amongst a limited, local group ensured its escape from the fate that befell so many other places of ancient worship. Another explanation – and the one which seems to make the most sense in human terms – is the unusually permissive attitude that has endured in this corner of Italy since it was first colonised by the Greeks in the ninth century BCE, and is a fundamental part of its past.

Transgression has been a part of Naples' identity for millennia, long before it gained an international reputation as a den of mafia sin and prohibitive danger. Originally a Greek town, Naples clung to its Eastern roots, and as early as the first century BCE it was the place to which wealthy and powerful Romans escaped for their little fix of 'Greek living'. Not that Naples was associated with moral laxity, it simply played by different rules, and these were emphatically not the quasi-impossible standards of moral perfection demanded of the ideal Roman citizen. An illuminating example is that of the unruly (to say the least) Emperor Nero. The Roman historian Suetonius[2] relates how the exhibitionist aspect of Nero's character reached its apex when he underwent a Neapolitan 'marriage'. Although Nero already had a wife in Rome he escaped accusations of polygamy because his betrothed was a young boy. Nero had apparently castrated the child before 'actually trying to make a woman out of him', dressing him up in a dress and veil, and whisking him off from Naples to Greece for a rather unorthodox honeymoon.

Was it Naples' link with Greece and the Orient that fitted it for its role as the Romans' pleasure garden, or was there another element that contributed to what has always been an outstanding level of cultural tolerance? Surely it has something to do with Vesuvius, the great 'question mark in the sky' which dominates the city. It

---

[2]. Not the most trustworthy of historians, but certainly a very good storyteller.

sits on the near horizon, threateningly familiar; a permanent promise that nothing is predictable, that life cannot be controlled, that the joy of today is worth more than ten indefinite tomorrows.

It is difficult to live next to a monster and remain impervious to the unpredictable throes of fate that it can create. Or certainly this is how it feels in Naples, where those who have made it to old age look somewhat startled, even disappointed to have done so. And well they might, in a city where motorbike helmets are slung casually over the shoulder rather than on the head, and where an entire apartment block may suddenly discover that the reason why so many of them have developed cancer is because the local mafia has been storing asbestos in their basement for the past twenty-five years.

Or maybe tolerance is just an extension of chaos, for there is no doubt that it is in chaos that the Neapolitans thrive. Quiet? It's anathema to them. Even the typography of the city is confusing. It rolls itself along its famous curving bay, flirting with the boats, and then stacks back up the hill, rising steeply from the sea as if hunching its shoulders over its damaged and slightly dilapidated historical heart. The steepness of the streets lends the buildings a strange sense of proportion, as though they were trying to flatten out the skyline, so that *palazzi* by the sea reach up to compete with the hills and dwarf cars, people and streets with a bulk so massive that even their terracotta pink walls look grey. Halfway up the hill things begin to shrink. You can look over the edge of a road and see below a borough that is itself a city in miniature, and which, complete with a bird's eye view of a church cupola, looks like a snow shaker, as if you were seeing it through glass. In effect you are, because like the rest of Naples it exists in another universe, and pays attention to rules that you will never understand and never risk understanding. Even as you drive onwards along the main road, back down, around the bay and up the next hill, the whole city disappears so swiftly that it's already a postcard, a vista, an unreality; and the tortuous, heavy streets of the twisted centre glisten in your memory and lose the looming darkness that turns even pigeons into threats and lends the subtlest of transactions a transgressive thrill.

¶ As an outsider it is relatively easy to accept chaotic Neapolitan life and moral open-mindedness. This, however, is more of a challenge for the Church, which considers the gays and the *femminielli* to be an irredeemably sinful group. This would not be a such problem were this not the group with whom the Church has to share its beloved icon at Montevergine. In 2002 the situation overwhelmed Archbishop Tarcisio Nazzaro, who was officiating at the shrine. Unable to hear himself above the shaking of cymbals and the stamping of feet, he lost his temper, grabbed a speakerphone, and began publicly berating the Madonna's less orthodox followers: 'Shame!' he yelled. 'You are shaming the Church! You are worse than the money changers! I will chase you from this temple!' His targets merely fluttered about in disarrayed rage, loving the spectacle. They were right not to be afraid: a few days later he was forced by a younger cohort of priests to retract what he had said, issuing instead a statement welcoming this 'very special' cohort of followers, and humbly asking that they be a little less exhibitionist when they come to visit the Madonna, who was offended by the noise and 'required respect'.

The Archbishop's retreat was a triumph for the *femminielli*, but not so much as events the following year. Rather than discouraging his unorthodox flock, the Archbishop had unwittingly highlighted what many in Italy consider to be the stranglehold of the Church. In 2003 the gay contingent of the crowd was considerably greater than it ever had been before, and hundreds of protestors arrived in Montevergine to show their support.

Most of the supporters were predictable: young and male, holding large billboards with images of male bodies and slogans demanding a 'free state and free love'. The interesting element was the fairly numerous older contingent. When I spoke to an elderly lady named Rosa, who would look more at home on a cookbook cover than at a gay pride march, she shook her majestically rounded, softly bearded chin: 'But this is our history, this is Naples' heritage. Our soul is dying with the *femminielli* – Naples is ceasing to exist.' I considered this to be a rather idiosyncratic, even melodramatic point of view. Until I heard it repeated again, and again, and again: 'The foreigners are taking over.'

'Our community is in crisis...'

'Where have all the *femminielli* gone?'

Naples has the most churches of any city in Italy (which is no mean feat), but it seems that this is not enough: there is a tenacious desire to hang on to a sense of identity that is based on the antique past. As the Neapolitans feel increasingly threatened – by poverty; by immigration; by the mafia; by the inevitable loss of community that is the fate of almost every major modern city; and by the very nature of change itself – they increasingly romanticise the *femminielli*. The values of openness and tolerance that this anomalous group embodies are a part of the Neapolitan character, which many feel is in decline.

¶ When we eventually walk into the church it is like walking into a cave: very dark, with thousands of candles giving off tiny aureoles of light that bob, seemingly disembodied, down the aisle.

Two *femminielli* enter. They look uncomfortable, and glance at each other with the solemnity of children, taking slow steps to keep pace with the crowd flowing down the nave. They tug their coats across their low-cut, leopard-printed chests. The shuffling silence is broken with a grave, low chant: '*Gloria, Gloria, in excelsis deum.*' Each person anoints a towering candelabrum with their individual offering of light. A priest casts a disparaging (unnoticed) glance at a journalist who is flashing his camera at the *femminielli*. The journalist is distracting the priest but only the priest is upset – everyone else is intent on the altar. The *femminielli* are without their accustomed audience – perhaps this is why they are suddenly united in self-consciousness.

Although the church pews are packed, there is nothing static about proceedings. I drift along the northern aisle of the church, my eyes flickering, like everybody else's, towards the great icon of the Madonna high above the altar. There are people everywhere, but apart from a general draw in her direction, there seems to be no logic to their movement, and certainly no focus. There is some kind of Mass going on, and two beautiful disembodied voices, one male, one female, sing out to one another, calling across the church to Mamma Schiavona. Other than that I cannot work out the logic: candle-clutching worshippers are hissed at by official-looking men in black; priests sporadically chant and pray; pilgrims fight their way to donate their blobs of light. Above it all the Madonna looks on, as impassive and beautiful as she is on every other day of the year.

When we walk out of the church it is to a renewed frenzy of activity. There is the sense of reckless lightness that comes just before an overdue holiday. Rather like coming out of the cinema in the middle of the day, I expect the valley to be dark, but the sun is still glaring off the snow, and balloons are still blazing in technicolour above the crowd. The oriental-sounding warble of Angelo's voice echoes all across the piazza, reverberating from the moustached mouths of young men and old ladies.

I wonder what the Virgin would make of the noisy crowd now dancing on this sacred spot. Would she be horrified or delighted? Certainly most of the conservative-seeming congregation appears to fully support the more outrageous behaviour that is now entering the stage. One woman just laughs and gestures to the church: 'For the Madonna it's always a party. You sing the songs from your heart or not at all.' Then the icon comes into view. She is ugly, broken and utterly serene as she bobs over the heads of the large assorted crowd that has come to sing her praises. The woman looks at her with adoration. So do the *femminielli*, and so do the priests. The contradictions seem extraordinary, but then again, perhaps this is what makes this celebration, such as it is, an inevitability.

I

INTERVIEW

WITH

WILLIAM BOYD

ON A WET, GREY MORNING IN MARCH, WILLIAM BOYD INVITED US INTO A LARGE TERRACED HOUSE, HALFWAY BETWEEN KING'S ROAD AND THE THAMES. On the right-hand side of the thin corridor's crisp white walls hang three dozen framed figurative paintings of identical size, each no bigger than a paperback book. These are David Hockney's series of flower sketches, executed on tablet computers and smart phones.

The enthusiasm which William Boyd shows for these is in keeping with the evident pleasure he takes in a range of creative arts – his career contains numerous film and television credits, alongside his notorious foray into the art world as the 'lost' Abstract Expressionist painter Nat Tate's biographer. Having authored a monograph in 1998 on Tate, backed by stellar co-conspirators David Bowie and Gore Vidal, he convinced many in the art world of the existence of this entirely fictitious artist who had supposedly killed himself at the age of thirty-two in 1960 – in the style of Hart Crane, by jumping off a boat – after destroying 99 per cent of his work. Opposite Hockney's digital *essais* sat a solitary Nat Tate, painted in preparation for the hoax by Boyd himself a decade or so ago.

The interview took place in an excessively heated first-floor living room; paintings in various styles cluttered the walls, illuminated by tall bay windows. On the coffee table were stacks of books, six or seven high – Robert Musil's THE MAN WITHOUT QUALITIES and Lewis Crofts' THE PORNOGRAPHER OF VIENNA prominent among them – testament to the meticulous research that goes into the composition of a William Boyd novel. His next novel, set in Freud's Vienna, will be his eleventh in a career spanning three decades that also includes several short story collections and volumes of non-fiction.

Perhaps his most ambitious projects have been the trilogy of works that tasked themselves with chronicling entire human lives, beginning with THE NEW CONFESSIONS. This includes his most celebrated novel, ANY HUMAN HEART, which tracks the course of its hero Logan Mountstuart through the chaos of the twentieth century. Boyd's life seems comparatively easy compared to those of his characters, who are often caught up in the vicissitudes of their times. Open and affable, William Boyd is a charming host, generous in his answers and parading a contagious enthusiasm for his work and the wider world of books.

Q. THE WHITE REVIEW — You grew up in Africa. What was that like?

A. WILLIAM BOYD — I am a child of the colonial system, and, as somebody said to me the other day, I suppose I am the last of a generation. I was born in Accra in 1952. Ghana got its independence in 1957 when I was five and then we moved to Nigeria, which got its independence in 1960, so we were really living out there at the tail end of the colonial era, when the wind of change was blowing through Africa.

My father was a doctor and my mother was a teacher and they spent their working lives out on what was then called the Gold Coast, where they moved in 1950. During the war, my father had specialised in tropical medicine, so he went back to the tropics five years later. It was supposed to be short-term but in fact he spent thirty years there, until he became ill and died. I grew up in a nice house with lots of African servants, nannies, gardeners, houseboys and cooks, and I often wonder how totally different my life would have been if my father had stayed and become a GP in Scotland.

It was an idyllic childhood, going to the beach and the club and the pool and tennis and so on, except in the late 1960s Nigeria began to implode. There were a series of military coups followed by the Nigerian Civil War – the Biafran War – which made a profound impression on me in my late teens. I was never in any danger but living in a country that was tearing itself apart was pretty extraordinary.

The great thing about the West African colonies as opposed to the eastern or the southern colonies was that there was no white settler class, so there was no racism. Obviously, apartheid existed in South Africa, but Rhodesia, Nyasaland, Kenya and Tanganyika had all been settled by white people and the tension between white and black was always there. Growing up in West Africa was, racially, a completely different experience. It was totally integrated and I could go anywhere without fearing anything whatsoever. I could walk around in the middle of the night in Ibadan, a great sprawling Nigerian city of close to a million people, and people would shout 'White Boy!' but you never felt threatened.

When I meet people who grew up in South Africa or Kenya, I realise that their experience of African life was quite different because of this settler-indigenous schism. But in West Africa it just wasn't there. White people would come out, work for thirty years, and then go away again. Nobody bought property, nobody had farms, nobody owned anything. In Rhodesia, there was this extraordinary statistic: 5 per cent of the white population owned 70 per cent of the arable land. In West Africa, that time bomb didn't exist.

When I look back on this childhood now, I see it as something quite extraordinary but of course where you live with your parents is quite normal. It was a very odd mix of the exotic and the astonishing and sometimes the frightening and the terrifying – all of these part of your everyday life.

Until the age of about twenty-two, I regarded West Africa as my home. Even though I was at boarding school and my relatives lived in Scotland, my home was in Western Nigeria, and I felt more at home there than I did in London or Edinburgh.

Q. THE WHITE REVIEW —— Did you feel comfortable when you were back in Scotland?
A. WILLIAM BOYD —— Not really. I felt sort of an outsider, which became useful to me as a writer. I spent nine and a half years at boarding school up in the north of Scotland, at Gordonstoun. I knew that world fantastically well but I realised quite early on it was totally artificial and bore no resemblance to the real world. The single-sex boarding school is a very strange society, and in my day you went there for a three-month stretch and it was a type of penal servitude.

I only saw the 'real' world on occasional holidays. I always felt as if I were on the outside looking in. I didn't feel particularly at home and it wasn't until I went to university and I started living in a flat in Glasgow that I could honestly say for the first time that I was experiencing British life.

My father was a powerful figure in his realm in Africa, where he ran half a dozen clinics and was responsible for 40,000 people, but I always remember him trying to buy an evening newspaper in Edinburgh. He didn't know what the money was and the paper man had to pick the coins out of his hands. Suddenly

I realised that he was adrift here as well.

Q. THE WHITE REVIEW — Is this why this idea of the outsider recurs in your writing?

A. WILLIAM BOYD — I do feel deracinated and I always have, and maybe that feeds into the way I write and my ability to look at society and the things around me with the slightly curious eye of the permanent visitor. It was a very long time before I wrote a novel that could be described as British. Obviously, parts of my novels were British, but I think the first truly home-based novel was my seventh, ARMADILLO, which is a London novel. My characters are often outsiders, or, because of events that happen to them, they become alien or under stress. Very often I put a central character in an environment that is strange, threatening, perplexing. I suspect that's as a result of my own journey through the various societies that I've encountered.

Q. THE WHITE REVIEW — Did you feel the need to write A GOOD MAN IN AFRICA to deal with your colonial childhood?

A. WILLIAM BOYD — Partly, although A GOOD MAN IN AFRICA was actually the fourth novel I'd written. I'd already written three unpublished novels. When I was an undergraduate I wrote a novel which was incredibly autobiographical about my year in France between school and university. I'd gone to do a diploma at the University of Nice, which was a very formative year for me. Again, I was away from my family, culture and language, and I wrote a novel about that year, got it out of my system, and put it in a bottom drawer where it remains.

Then I wrote a novel about the Biafran War while studying at Oxford, where I was doing my D.Phil. It was a very self-consciously modernist novel with a fractured form, using diary extracts, newspaper extracts, standard narrative and first person. I'd shattered the linear conventions of the novel but it didn't quite come off so I wrote another novel – a thriller – because I was beginning to get a bit desperate about getting published.

At the time, I was also publishing short stories quite successfully – nine or ten appeared in magazines and some were being broadcast on the radio. My short story writing career seemed to be going well, so I sent a collection off to Hamish Hamilton and Jonathan Cape. In a post scriptum, I told them that I'd written a novel featuring a character called Morgan Leafy, a fat drunken diplomat in Africa who appeared in two of the stories.

Very quickly, I got a letter back from Hamish Hamilton asking for more information about the novel I had mentioned, so I wrote the synopsis of this novel in three or four pages and sent it off. A letter came back saying they'd like to publish my short story collection and my novel. That was the great 'Yes!' punch-the-air day, but they wanted to publish the novel first, and, of course, I hadn't written it, I had lied.

So I said to my new editor, Christopher Sinclair-Stevenson, 'Look, the manuscript is in a shocking state, I just need a couple of months to knock it into shape', and I sat down and wrote A GOOD MAN IN AFRICA in a white heat of dynamic endeavour in three months at my kitchen table. I was teaching at Oxford at the time so I just dropped everything and borrowed some money from my mother. It was all there waiting to come out and suddenly there it was.

Six months later, the stories came out. I published two books in 1981, so it was a great start, but it was by no means an overnight success. I was able to write A GOOD MAN IN AFRICA because I'd already written three novels. It's not the classic first novel because I'd already written that four or five years earlier. I'd gotten the fascination with my own life out of my system.

Q. THE WHITE REVIEW — Are there no autobiographical elements there? What about Dr Alex Murray, the good man in Africa? Is he not based on your father?

A. WILLIAM BOYD — It is very much the world I knew. It is completely set in Ibadan in Western Nigeria even though I changed the names, but everybody in it is made up. It's rooted in my autobiography in terms of its colour, texture and smells but the story is – and that's something that's always been the case with me – invented.

There is an autobiographical element in that the character of Dr Murray is very much a two-dimensional portrait of my father. He had died the year before I wrote the novel so he was very much present in my mind. The clash in the novel is between a dissolute, overweight diplomat and the rectitude and solidity of somebody rather like my father. It may echo the clash which he and I had. We got on pretty well, but we were like chalk and cheese. So, there is an element of my own life in it but it's 70 per cent out of my imagination.

Q. THE WHITE REVIEW — Who were the authors who were influencing you at the time, and throughout your career? When reading your books, one is so often reminded of Evelyn Waugh.

A. WILLIAM BOYD — I'm fascinated by Waugh and I've read everything he's written but I'm almost more fascinated by him as a type of Englishman. The absolute blackness and ruthlessness of his sense of humour is something that chimes with me. I don't think BRIDESHEAD REVISITED, A HANDFUL OF DUST and SWORD OF HONOUR are as good or as brilliant as his early comedies. I'd also read Kingsley Amis and I think I am a comic novelist in the sense that I see the world as an absurd and curious place.

As for other writers, I studied and later taught English literature at Oxford so I read my way through the canon. I was also reading a lot of American literature at the time. In fact, if you'd asked me then I would probably have said I preferred Philip Roth, John Updike, Joseph Heller or Ernest Hemingway to their English equivalents. I was widely read when I was first published but not conscious of any influence, although the comic-realistic tradition in English fiction is so strong, it's such a broad river, that I am bound to have picked up influences along the way.

I've always read voraciously and indiscriminately and I apparently started reading very early. My father was a great reader of detective novels and when I came back to Africa on my school holidays, there would be a great stack of little 220-page detective novels. Some were interesting – Raymond Chandler, Ed McBain, Georges Simenon – and many others are completely forgotten like Richard S. Prather and Peter Cheyney. I would read my way through ten or twenty of them in the holidays and then go back to Jane Austen.

Q. THE WHITE REVIEW — Why did you decide to become a writer?

A. WILLIAM BOYD — I wanted to be a painter originally because I was very good at art when I was young. I did O-Level and A-Level Art and I was very keen. It was my first love, and I think I knew that I was not cut out for any kind of proper job. I come from a family of middle-class professional Scots – engineers, doctors, lawyers, accountants – but I somehow got this idea that I wanted to be an artist. I told my father I was thinking about going to art school, but he just said, 'Forget it, not a hope in hell.' So, not being a rebel, I just switched to another art form – literature.

If I had gone to art school, I may have been a very mediocre painter, but as a writer I always had the safety net of an academic career if it all went pear-shaped. It was only after I'd published three books and written a film that I decided that I could quit my job as a college lecturer at Oxford. By then I felt that I could cut all these ties to live by my wits and my pen, but for a while I wasn't sure if I could earn a living out of writing, which is a key dilemma in a writer's life.

Q. THE WHITE REVIEW —— What kind of process was involved in becoming a writer?

A. WILLIAM BOYD —— When I was at university in Glasgow I wrote a novel, a play and some poetry. I also wrote a lot of theatre criticism and film criticism for the university newspaper. When I moved to Oxford, I went to work for *Isis* and I met other writers because the place was full of them. Iris Murdoch lived up the road; I lived next door to Brian Aldiss, the science-fiction writer; and I entered a short story competition that Roald Dahl was judging. I also met other students with dreams of writing such as Andrew Motion, Alan Hollinghurst, A.N. Wilson and James Fenton.

We were at the beginning of our careers and that collegiate feeling of young writers wanting to make their way in the world helped. I started to review for little magazines – BOOKS & BOOKMEN and THE LONDON MAGAZINE – and then I got a review in the TIMES LITERARY SUPPLEMENT, another red letter day. I was slowly but surely finding my way into that world and discovering the nuts and bolts of being a writer. It was an education but it took several years before it finally bore fruit and I had that first published book in my hands.

Q. THE WHITE REVIEW —— How do you go about writing? Have you always written in the same way?

A. WILLIAM BOYD —— Yes, I have actually. I'm part of that pre-computer generation and I've always written in longhand. All my novels have manuscripts, which is rare for anybody under the age of 40. I used to write my first draft in my tiny anal retentive handwriting and then I'd write a fair copy in large legible handwriting. I would then give that second draft to a typing agency – that dates me – and the typists typed it up from my fair copy so that I could then hand it in to the publisher. I've always had this process of writing a draft and then writing it all again, however long it takes. Now, of course, I type the second draft onto a screen.

Q. THE WHITE REVIEW —— How much changes between drafts?

A. WILLIAM BOYD —— I change things all the time. When you are copying a sentence or typing it or rewriting it you think, 'Oh, this is clumsy', or 'I can stick that word here', so the difference from manuscript to typescript or manuscript to fair copy is often huge. It's a very good editorial process and I wonder if writers who write directly onto a screen lose that. Of course, you rewrite and polish anyway, but there's something about the two forms, there's a real moment of decision, and just making that transfer, I wouldn't change that working method now. I do write screenplays straight onto the screen, I do write journalism straight onto the screen, but I would never write a novel or a short story like that, I just seem to need the two forms – the handwritten and then the perfection of type.

The last few months of my working life have been very simple: I get up in the morning and write. I can write for about three hours and then I'm knackered but I can type up what I've written. I've been doing that seven days a week. I've been writing my latest novel since the early summer of last year and since December I've been working full-time seven days a week on it. I'm now polishing it and tweaking it but I'm already thinking about the next one and that makes me relaxed because that plane is circling and waiting to be called in to land.

Q. THE WHITE REVIEW — Do you have a structure worked out when you sit down to write?

A. WILLIAM BOYD — Yes. It takes me about three years to complete a novel; I spend roughly two years figuring it out and one year writing it. Iris Murdoch, who worked in the same way, called it the period of invention and the period of composition. I think that's quite a neat division. It's become absolutely rigid for me now.

I get an idea for a novel, which is usually one sentence or a concept. Then I spend a long time thinking about it, filling out notebooks, travelling, acquiring the library I need for the book. I set about making more and more elaborate plans for the narrative and making lots and lots of mistakes, going up blind alleys and developing characters or sub-themes that fizzle out. Even then, I haven't actually started writing the book. That whole period of invention is absolutely crucial in my work. Eventually, and usually when I know how the book is going to end, I will write a draft of the last paragraph or the last few lines – so I'm that sure of it – and only at that stage do I write chapter one and start the book.

Then it takes me about nine months or a year to write it but I write with confidence – not particularly fast but with fluency because I'm not stopping to think, 'What happens next?' I've already made all those mistakes and all of those bad decisions and corrected them. Of course, I still get lots of new ideas as I'm writing but there's a real template, or as I describe it a skeleton, and then I add the flesh when I write it.

Q. THE WHITE REVIEW — Do you play around with the voice of your characters in the invention period?

A. WILLIAM BOYD — Yes, because those elements are the first questions you ask yourself once you've got your idea and the whole process of invention is a series of questions and answers that goes on over this period of two years. For example, I ask myself whether it is going to be in the first person or the third person, and that decision is absolutely crucial. Am I going to write from one point of view or from many points of view? Is my central character going to be male or female? The answers to these questions trigger a whole set of other questions: 'Oh, it's a woman, right, OK, how old is she? What's her name? How tall is she?' And so on and so forth and this aggregate of information begins to accrue and you see stories and storylines emerging.

Q. THE WHITE REVIEW — What are you currently working on?

A. WILLIAM BOYD — It's a novel that starts in Vienna in 1913 and it's about a young Englishman who is an actor. He's got a sexual dysfunction and he's engaged to be married, so he decides to go out to Vienna to try out this newfangled psychoanalysis lark to see if it can cure him of this particular problem. He starts being psychoanalysed and he meets another woman there and then, because it's one of my novels, things go from bad to worse and World

War I begins.

It is very long, and it is also possibly one of my most complex plots because he gets embroiled in all sorts of Buchanesque adventures, but it's got a lot more sex in it than John Buchan ever had. It covers a lot of ground but I now realise, two weeks before I hand it in to my editor, that it's actually about lying and uncertainty which seems to me to be a very modern state of mind. And with Vienna in 1913–1914, we are at the beginning of the modern era and in the capital of a decadent empire. Something about the city then made it the focus and locus of what was modern.

Q. THE WHITE REVIEW — How do you go about researching your novels? Do you read a lot?

A. WILLIAM BOYD — Yes, I often read novels set in the period I want to write about. For this latest novel, for example, I read Joseph Roth and Robert Musil. I find novels very useful because what a novelist saw in 1912 or 1913 is not necessary what a historian writing today will see. I also use photographs a lot. I've never really gone beyond the twentieth century – 1902 is as early a novel as I have set – so photographic evidence exists and I find books of photographs fantastically helpful. Then I use all sorts of newspapers, magazines, guidebooks – but all contemporary.

It's not about reading some book on the Viennese Secession, it's about reading books that are much more banal because as a novelist the banal is what you are looking for. What struck Joseph Roth as he described a country scene in THE RADETZKY MARCH is what I want to reproduce through the eyes of this young Englishman in Vienna for the first time. It's a very selective process and if you get the detail right suddenly that world comes alive. As you sift through this material you find that you are not looking at it in the way that a journalist or a historian would look at it – you are looking at it for something that intrigues and seems unusual.

Take the business of communicating for example: you could make telephone calls in 1914–15 but only 20,000 people had telephones. The telegram and the telegraph offices were the main avenues for communication because you just popped one in the post at half a pence a word. These details make the book come alive but they have to be fed in seamlessly so that it doesn't look like a gobbet of research. We've all read novels where you plough through three pages on the manufacture of rubber and you realise that the writer has been to Singapore to see a rubber plantation and by God are we going to hear about it. It is a very interesting process to make it seem entirely natural and yet at the same time you want the reader to be aware of time travel.

I always quote something from ULYSSES where Bloom goes into a pub in Dublin and orders a glass of claret and a sardine sandwich. That seems very modern and it brings a Dublin pub to life in a way that knowing that Guinness costs one and sixpence doesn't. Language is another thing. People swore as violently in 1913 as they do today, maybe not in mixed company but amongst men, and certainly soldiers' language was as rich as anyone's.

Q. THE WHITE REVIEW — Where do you find traces of that? Because it doesn't appear much in the literature of the time...

A. WILLIAM BOYD — It does if you know where to look for it. I can give you two good examples. If you read the letters of James Joyce to Nora Barnacle, 1909 or thereabouts, they are the most sexually candid letters you can find two lovers writing to each other. Joyce was in Trieste and Nora was in Dublin so they wrote each other some dirty letters for sexual stimulation at a distance.

The other one is a novel by Frederic Manning which might be the best novel that came out of World War I. Manning wrote two versions of the book: one called MIDDLE PARTS OF FORTUNE which is unexpurgated and another called HER PRIVATES WE which had no swear words in it and was published at the time. Manning was an intellectual who fought at the Battle of the Somme as a private soldier. The soldiers he writes about are all saying 'fuck' and 'cunt' like a soldier today would, but of course our image of the Tommy is of a plucky chap with a fag in his mouth saying, 'Cor, blimey, it's the Huns throwing over.'

This is what is so fantastic about Manning's novel. You realise the soldiers didn't give a toss about the war, they hated their officers, they hated the officers back home, and the only things they wanted were food, drink and sex if it was available. These words weren't invented in 1940. You just need to read Shakespeare's soldiers to see that it's an absolute truth, but gentility has tended to mask that so it does take some unearthing.

Q. THE WHITE REVIEW — What was the genesis of your forthcoming novel on psychoanalysis?
A. WILLIAM BOYD —I became very interested in psychoanalysis, which is one of the three great scientific revolutions. There is the Copernican revolution, when we realised that the sun didn't go around us but that we went around the sun. There's the Darwinian revolution – we are animals – and then there's the Freudian revolution – half the time we don't know why we do things because our unconscious mind is at work.

Whatever anyone may think of Freud and however discredited he is, there is no doubt that we are all Freudians. Even though the unconscious existed before Freud, he schematised and systematised it and changed the way we think about ourselves. So to begin with I asked myself, 'What would it have been like to be psychoanalysed and to realise that half the things you do are driven by forces that you are only partially aware of?' Then I decided I'd send my protagonist off to Vienna before World War I when psychoanalysis was new and controversial, and off I went.

That was the idea that grabbed me and it's nearly always like that. I start off with an idea and it has enough mass in it to be a 400- or 500-page novel. The ideas I get for short stories or movies or a piece I might write are different. There is a certain category of idea I get which is gravid enough or has enough potential to fill a novel. I've never written a short novel.

Some people like to start and see where they end up, but I'm not that kind of writer. I like to know my destination and my period of composition is not fraught with having to stop and invent, which is where novels get abandoned of course. The first sixty pages come like that and then you think, 'What does she do next?' I've never abandoned a novel because I never get to that stage.

Q. THE WHITE REVIEW — Some writers say that once they start writing their characters take on a life of their own and become uncontrollable.
A. WILLIAM BOYD — Vladimir Nabokov was always asked this and he was very much anti-Freudian and anti the unconscious. He said: 'All my characters are galley slaves and I'm the man on the deck with the whip.' I feel rather like that because I try to make my characters live and breathe on the page as real and complex human beings. You are the master of that particular world and they are your creatures. Sometimes you don't

know where you get ideas from but it's not the character taking over. That's a romantic fallacy or convention — the inspired driven artist at the mercy of his or her muse. I think writing a novel takes so long that there is something very dogged and methodical about it. I believe in the Flaubertian-Joycean model of the artist controlling everything, not the drink-fuelled spontaneity of the muse descending.

Q. THE WHITE REVIEW — How does that relate to when you are writing about characters who are already iconic figures such as Woolf, Picasso, Hemingway or Joyce? How do you create their voice?

A. WILLIAM BOYD — They are usually people I have been very intrigued by anyway and I've read a great deal about them. It's a kind of thought experiment. I think, 'What would it actually be like to meet Virginia Woolf?' I've never particularly liked Virginia Woolf and I've read everything and taught her books for many years but she just seems to me an unpleasant, snobbish, slightly bogus person. I know she was disturbed as well and that's how I imagined her.

If you read her letters and diaries, you see what type of person she is — we've all met them. The challenge as a writer is to bring that iconic figure alive in a way that makes them a real person rather than a postcard that you bought at the National Portrait Gallery. I've written stories about Chekhov, Wittgenstein, Brahms and Cyril Connolly, people I'm really intrigued by, and I try to make them live as characters in fiction. It's about stripping away the myth and getting to the real person, but they are always people about whom I have been curious about and read a lot about. I can't imagine writing a novel about George VI for example.

Q. THE WHITE REVIEW — The Duke of Windsor is much more interesting.

A. WILLIAM BOYD — Yes, and that is the wonderful thing about writing fiction. I got Logan Mountstuart to meet all these people that I was intrigued by so I could present them through his eyes. Some people who knew the Duke and Duchess of Windsor who I have spoken to have said that their appearance in ANY HUMAN HEART is a fascinating and very credible portrait of them. Some of my favourite short stories of mine are these biographical short stories because when it is successful I feel like I captured the essence of the person in those fifteen or twenty pages and the reader gets a sense of them as a character quite apart from their reputation.

Q. THE WHITE REVIEW — Does this tie in with your interest in blurring the lines between fact and fiction? Say with Nat Tate for example? Or is it really just a narrative device you are using?

A. WILLIAM BOYD — That exercise was to make something utterly fictitious seem completely real so that the line is blurred, so that your suspension of disbelief is rocky, and it's amazing how it could be done with tricks and presentation. And why did I do it? If you look at three books where I do this, THE NEW CONFESSIONS, NAT TATE and ANY HUMAN HEART — published between 1987 and 2002, so that's a long time — I think they stand up as a trilogy of books all exploring the same thing: is it true or is it false?

There is an ongoing argument that somehow non-fiction is more powerful and gripping than fiction and I felt that I wanted to reclaim the top of the hill for fiction. These three books were a series of attempts to prove that something made-up could supplant what you might regard as real.

Q. THE WHITE REVIEW — Is there a critique of the art world in the Nat Tate project?

A. WILLIAM BOYD — There is. I wrote the book in 1998, at the height of the Young British Artists phenomenon. I was on the editorial board of MODERN PAINTERS at the time and I was, in a way, answering that early urge to be a painter by writing about art. I've written a great deal about painting and artists and I have strong opinions about who's good and who isn't and it struck me that a lot of the YBAs who were being acclaimed and making vast sums of money were, when you judged them as artists, very average, not to say sub-average.

This also happened in the 1950s in New York with the Abstract Expressionists, who are the first group of artists who had that level of fame. Jackson Pollock was featured in LIFE magazine, which was unheard of, like a film star... When you look closely at the Abstract Expressionists you see that as figurative artists they are average. A lot of them couldn't draw to save their lives. Jackson Pollock's attempts to draw are lamentable and yet he is one of the most famous artists of the twentieth century.

After roughly a year of doing his action paintings, he started painting really crap semi-representational stuff, and I saw in those two moments how enormous acclaim seemed to blind people to the merits of the art being produced. NAT TATE is not a critique of any particular YBA, but more a kind of fable about an excess of fame attached to too modest a talent. Nat is a case in point, a perfectly OK painter, but when he comes up against a genius – a word to be used very rarely – like Georges Braque, it shines too harsh a light on what he does and he cracks and kills himself, having destroyed 99 per cent of all the work he had produced.

I think Pollock wanted to die because he couldn't live with his fame and he eventually deliberately crashed his car. A lot of these artists died unhappy and tormented – Basquiat is another who drugged himself to death. I think art has to be evaluated, there have to be criteria, otherwise what's the point? We are entitled to express our opinions and my own touchstone is virtuosity of some kind. I'm very interested in modern art and I think certain artists are fantastically gifted and intriguing, but then there are others who are even more famous who seem to me almost risibly bad, but such is the nature of the art world and the art market that the whole thing can function on the basis of four or five incredibly rich patrons, which seems to me very skewed.

I had a big argument in Germany when NAT TATE was published there last year with the editor of a German art magazine who said to me [speaks in German accent], 'I am obsessed with contemporary art!' He obviously thought I was some retro-throwback figure and I said, 'Well, I love contemporary art as well but I do judge it and I'm not going to just take everything.' There's a line in the film version of ANY HUMAN HEART where Ben Leeping says, 'I just bought an Andy Warhol the other day, incredibly expensive!' and Logan says, 'Yes, I call it snack art. You think you are satisfied but after an hour or so you are hungry again.'

In a way it's facetious but you can go to see these exhibitions and you get it, you know, you can get Damien Hirst, and you see what he's done, and then you set it in the context of contemporary art and think, 'Just how original is it?' and that's another matter. Vitrines have been around for a long long time, as have spin paintings. But is it as interesting as a small Georges Braque late landscape? That's the sort of question I ask myself, and I think, 'No', but I still find myself amused, beguiled, provoked by contemporary art. They're not snake-oil salesmen, but they seem to me smart

II

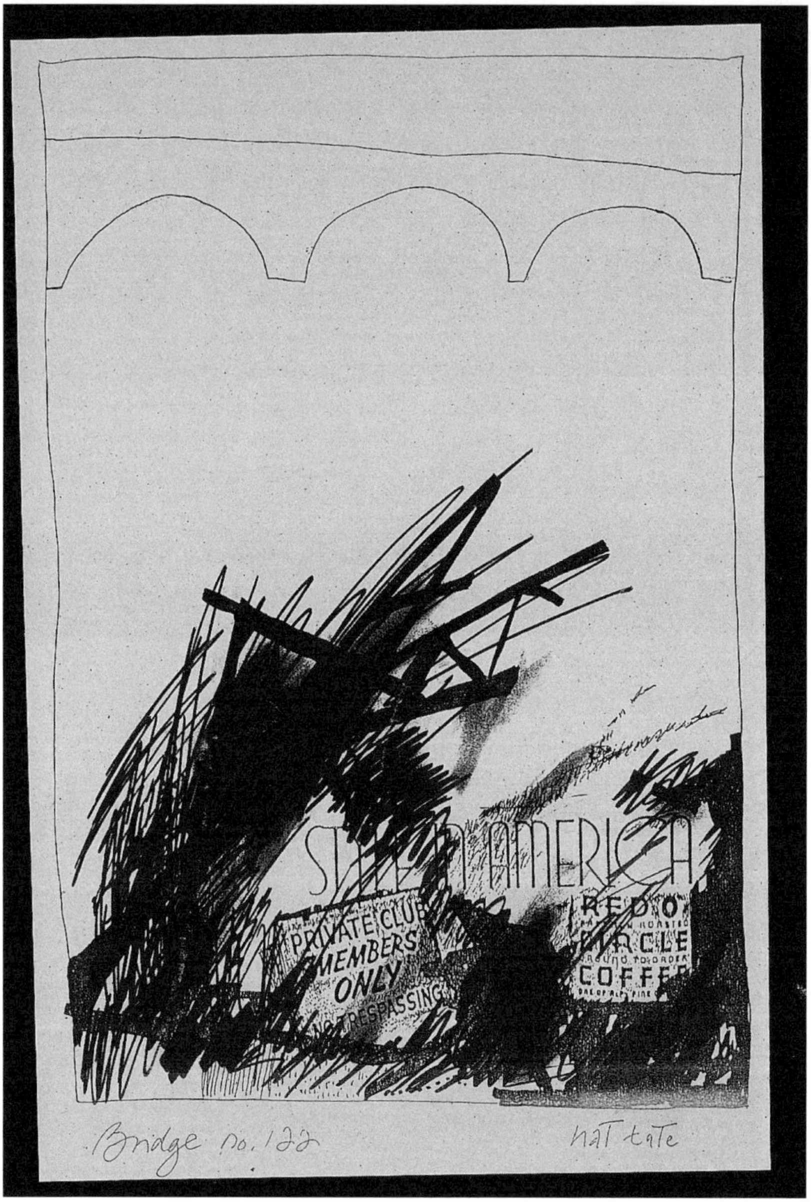
AMERICA
PRIVATE CLUB
MEMBERS
ONLY
RED O
CIRCLE
COFFE
Bridge no.122
nat tate

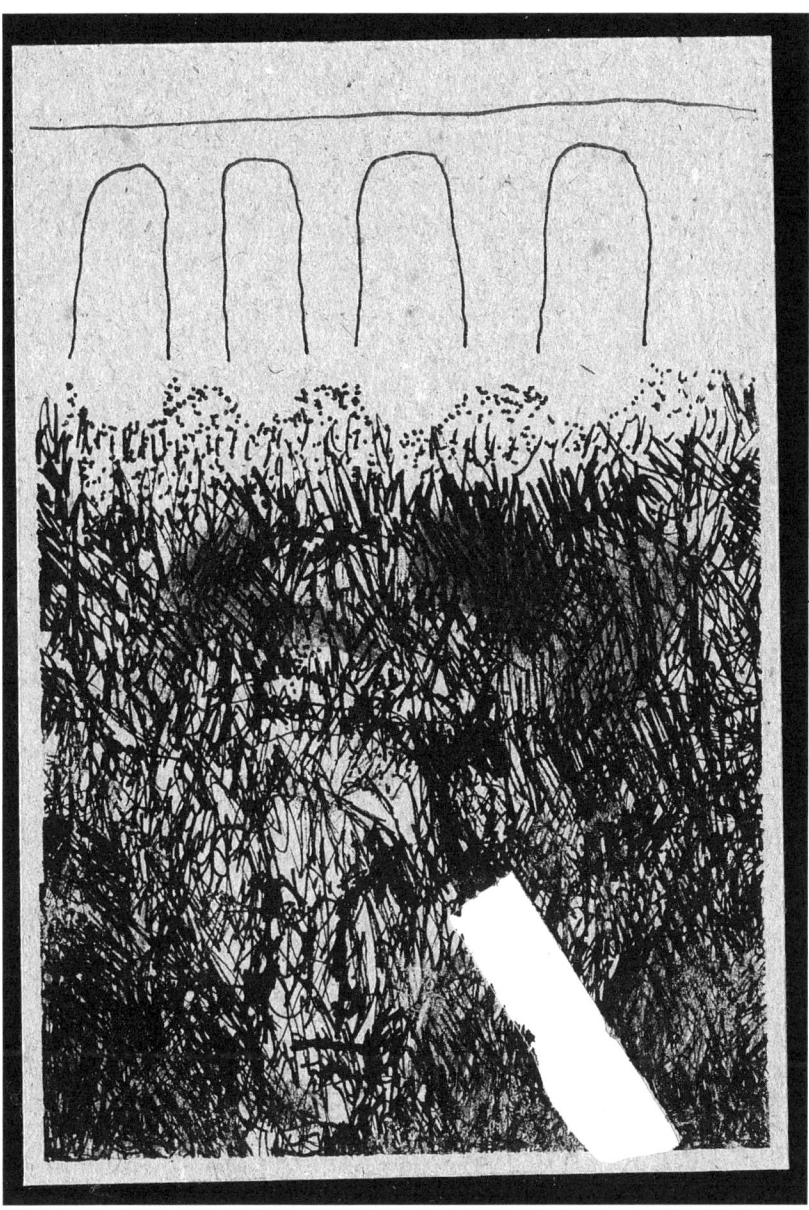

idea peddlers. When you go to art schools now all the students are thinking, 'What's my gimmick?', not, 'Can I draw a hand?' It's cyclical, and it will come back.

I was in The Wolseley the other night and there was Lucian Freud. I think he goes there almost every night. Nobody recognised him, this funny little man with paint-stained shoes who paints nudes. He's a figurative painter – Degas would have been able to claim him as a fellow artist – and conceivably our greatest living artist. I've also got to know David Hockney, that extraordinary painter and intellectual, a virtuoso who can draw phenomenally well. He sends me little iPhone pictures, absolutely stunning little figurative paintings. That's just my taste and the editor of the German art magazine would totally disagree with me and think I was old-fashioned, but I think judging work by the virtuosity on display is a very good system. If there isn't any on display, there have to be other things that make you evaluate it.

Q. THE WHITE REVIEW —— Is it true that you painted the Nat Tate paintings yourself?

A. WILLIAM BOYD —— Yes, they are all mine. Again, that's the frustrated artist in me. In fact, we're going to sell a Nat Tate at auction in June, I hope, so I've 'found' one in the attic...

Q. THE WHITE REVIEW —— What was the Nat Tate launch evening like? Were people really pretending that they had once known him?

A. WILLIAM BOYD —— Well I wasn't even there – can you believe it? – I was on a book tour. We were going to do two evenings. 1 April 1998 was Manhattan and then a week later we had a huge, equally glitzy party booked for London. I was going to be at the London party and I had given big interviews in national newspapers and on the radio talking about how I had discovered a forgotten artist.

The plan was to launch the book straight up, saying, 'Here's a book, a monograph by me about this forgotten artist.' I thought it might run until somebody might accuse me in three months time of making the whole thing up. Phase one was the launch in New York, which David Bowie, who was the publisher of the book and one of the key conspirators, arranged with his chum Jeff Koons to have in his huge studio in Manhattan. And of course, if Jeff Koons and David Bowie invite you to a party, you go, so they got everybody there.

There were very few conspirators. There was me, three people who had worked on the book, and Bowie. Even Koons didn't know. On his trip to cover the launch an English journalist named David Lister overheard a conversation about how it was all fake. He had bought it completely. He later claimed that he had been suspicious and went looking for the Janet Felzer Gallery on Madison Avenue and couldn't find it. Basically, he had been hoodwinked and believed that Nat Tate was an unknown Abstract Expressionist so he threw a hissy fit and to silence him we had to bring him into the inner circle.

Lister was the one that went around this glamorous Manhattan party with all the glitterati and the fashionistas saying – and we weren't planning on doing this at all – 'What do you think about Nat Tate?' Bowie read three extracts from the book, and he had actually written the blurb of the book saying he had known Nat Tate which was very convincing, and I got Gore Vidal and John Richardson, who was Picasso's biographer, to reminisce about him too. It was a very elaborate lie, a very carefully thought-out pretence, but Lister played agent provocateur by going around asking people about Nat and they'd say, 'Oh yeah, it's so sad, he died so young, and I think

I saw a show of his in...' and dug holes for themselves and jumped in.

Then, we were going to do exactly the same thing in London, but Lister realised he was sitting on a huge story and about three days after the Manhattan launch he blew it wide open in the *Independent* with a headline along the lines of: 'British Novelist Fools Manhattan Art World'.

I was in Paris on a book tour and I was quite pissed off because it had not been planned like that and I came back into a twenty-four-hour news maelstrom as everybody picked it up, which shows you that everybody loves a hoax, but who was hoaxed and for how long, that's a good question.

I was on Newsnight for twenty minutes interviewed by Paxman. I was interviewed around the world. With hindsight that was probably the best thing that could have happened. When the original book sold out and went out of print, I said to Bloomsbury, 'Why don't we reissue it?' and that's what we're doing this year. We're doing that auction in June to coincide with that and if somebody will pay money to own one, again, some sort of blurring between reality and the fictive has occurred.

Q. THE WHITE REVIEW —— You've written many different types of novels. *Restless*, for example, was a spy novel and had clear commercial potential. Do you write novels with the market in mind?

A. WILLIAM BOYD —— I have always cherry-picked my genres. I do believe that the novel is fundamentally about story and character and the more intriguing the story and the characters, the more beguiling the book. My novels have always had a very strong narrative line and often a very complex plot as well as everything else.

I became interested in spies and spying when I wrote *Any Human Heart* because Logan Mountstuart is a spy in the war, and I'd been reading a lot about Kim Philby, the master double agent, just wondering again, what must it have been like? From this, I thought I would write a novel following on from *Any Human Heart* about a spy, but I decided to make the spy a woman to refresh a tired old genre.

The Blue Afternoon had a serial killer mystery lurking at its centre. *Armadillo* is about a massive insurance fraud, borrowed from that corporate thriller world. It's the same thing with *Ordinary Thunderstorms* which is powered by that classic innocent man-on-the-run. *An Ice-Cream War* is a kind of chase – one brother following another. I've happily gone to genre to provide myself with the motor for my novel, and then around it constructed a rather elaborate and – I hope – beautiful automobile.

This new novel I'm just finishing is the third part in a trilogy following *Restless* and *Ordinary Thunderstorms*. It's the final panel in a triptych exploring how to take a genre and give it a different kind of energy, in the same way that *The New Confessions*, *Nat Tate* and *Any Human Heart* were pushing the boundaries of fiction into the world of the real and the documentary. There was no grand plan, it's just with hindsight I can see what's going on: I've taken ingredients that seemed familiar and given them a good shake-up.

Q. THE WHITE REVIEW —— Your characters are often beset by circumstances around them but they tend to find peace at the end of their novels, to end at ease.

A. WILLIAM BOYD —— I do make them fall back on their own resources as human beings. Whatever they've got, whether it's resources of character or ingenuity or particular skills, if they come through then, you're right, there is this sense in which they've proved themselves in a way that that they never imagined possible. I'm not doing this consciously, but I do give my protagonist in the new novel a really hard time. Maybe it's an exploration of the fragility of my own rather comfortable and easy life.

In ORDINARY THUNDERSTORMS, by sheer bad luck, Adam loses everything. Identity, passport, credit card – all the social buttresses we use to create our identity in the twenty-first century. I suppose you could go through all my books and see characters challenged by circumstance. In A GOOD MAN IN AFRICA, Morgan Leafy is blackmailed by a very clever African politician who asks him to corrupt a man who is incorruptible. Same in ARMADILLO, or with Logan. It's one of those tropes that all my books can be boiled down to – the character finds himself in a world he doesn't understand and has to somehow get through to the other side.

Q. THE WHITE REVIEW —— Is that why your characters drink so much?

A. WILLIAM BOYD —— Well, it's also a period thing. People drank a lot more liquor before. Maybe it's also a novelist's thing. All novelists are drinkers, some of them heavy drinkers. Anthony Burgess, who I knew, used to have a crate of gin delivered to his house once a week. Twelve bottles of gin a week! His wife was an alcoholic, but he kept up with her. Kingsley Amis was a bottle of whisky a night man, and Lawrence Durrell, Malcolm Lowry – there are many examples of the writer as drunk – let alone Scott Fitzgerald, Faulkner and Hemingway.

Alcohol is a very good way of fixing a period or fixing a character. Some of my characters are teetotal but drinking – I drink wine – is part of the texture of my life so it seems completely normal. When I'm writing about people, I ask myself, 'What are they doing with their hands?' There's quite a lot of smoking in my novels as well and I don't smoke and never have. It's a period thing. When did women start smoking in public? In 1913 it was rather daring but a lot of them smoked. Virginia Woolf smoked like a chimney, sixty a day. You forget that before the 1960s, before the cancer scare arrived, smoking was almost completely universal. I remember flying back from Africa as a 7- or 8-year-old and the entire plane seemed to be full of smokers. Proust was recommended that he smoke cigarettes to ease his asthma. It's part of the textures of life in a given period.

Q. THE WHITE REVIEW —— One gets a sense that you see history as inexplicable and the lives of individuals as a series of coincidences.

A. WILLIAM BOYD —— I think that old saying, 'All history is the history of unintended consequences' rings very true. The overriding theme of ANY HUMAN HEART is that all our lives are governed by luck. Any life is the sum of all the good luck and bad luck you've had and some manifestly had a lot of good luck or bad luck but with most people it sort of evens out over the course of threescore years and ten.

That world view is entirely plausible but it's faithless. There's no deity so it is your human experience and your human predicament ultimately and you'd better make the most of it while you can. That's very much my own view of life. There's a sense that your present happiness, whatever that may be, is actually an incredibly fragile thing and most of us can't bear to think about that but it's quite good to have it at the back of your mind because it does govern the way you make decisions. That contentment or that stasis of happiness can be shattered at any moment. If you believe in a god or gods, then there's a whole other story, but if you don't you're stuck in the present moment keeping your fingers crossed, advancing with due caution. That's how I approach life and I dare say it colours the way I write about my fictional lives as well.

I recognised this very early on in Evelyn Waugh. His sense of humour is so ruthless that he won't reward his characters with what they deserve. Instead, he will follow the implacable dice-throwing rules of the universe. At the end of an early travel book called LABELS, which he wrote as his first marriage was collapsing, his main character says, 'Fortune is the least capricious of deities, and arranges things on the just and rigid system that no one should be very happy for very long.' It's not about being nihilistic or cynical, it's just about realising that good luck is as likely as bad luck.

Q. THE WHITE REVIEW — It seems that, through your godless perspective on the world, you have evolved your own moral system which you impose on your characters, whereby humans are depicted as flawed beings but capable of redemption on their own.

A. WILLIAM BOYD — Yes, I think that's absolutely true. What do you base a moral system on once you remove the deity issue from your scheme of things? There seem to me to be very simple adages that people have known for millennia, 'Do as you will be done by', 'Love is better than no love', or 'Being loved and loving in return is fuller than anything you will experience'. Although I don't articulate it in such a crude way, it powers a lot of my fiction. In ORDINARY THUNDERSTORMS, even though Adam has killed a man and is now a hospital porter with a false name, his life is made bearable by the fact that it has Rita in it and their love is shared. I don't offer that to all my characters.

If I was a devout Anglo-Catholic, no doubt my fiction would be different. One of my favourite scenes in the film version of ANY HUMAN HEART is when Peter Scabius says he's converted to Catholicism. Logan is, as it were, speaking for me when he says, 'It's all mumbo-jumbo mate.' Scabius is having nothing of it and the two of them clash over it. It's a really interesting microcosm of two attitudes to the human predicament. Scabius is completely bogus of course.

Q. THE WHITE REVIEW — Scabius is an interesting character. Is he based on anyone?

A. WILLIAM BOYD — Someone wrote to me from the Graham Greene society to ask whether Scabius was based on him. Scabius stumbles into a marriage, has two children, didn't love his wife, gets a job at a provincial newspaper as Greene did, writes these techies and then hits gold with GUILT. Then he becomes a portentous and rather heavyweight novelist. The other thing about him is that he's a pure egomaniac and you don't meet many of them. I've only met half a dozen. They don't have to be famous or rich but all they think about is themselves and the world only exists in so far as they see it from the glow they cast. Scabius is one of those people who is oblivious of his own monstrous ego. These people are actually very funny when you encounter them because you can never dent their self-assurance. They're absolutely impregnable.

Scabius is a poor man's Graham Greene in a way. Greene is someone I'm really interested in as a writer and as a case study. His Catholicism seems to me to be a complete sham, just like Muriel Spark, another writer I really admire who converted to Catholicism.

Waugh's conversion, on the other hand, was genuine – he needed it – whereas the other two I think did it and then found it useful to be 'Catholic Novelists'. I've read a great deal about both Muriel Spark and Graham Greene and they seem to me to be the most irreligious people I can imagine. They paid lip service to religion but it doesn't wash with me.

Q THE WHITE REVIEW —— Have you ever seen yourself fictionalised in a contemporary's work?

A. WILLIAM BOYD —— No, I haven't, and I don't draw on life in that straightforward causal way. I've been reading about H. G. Wells and Henry James recently. Wells wrote a novel at the end of James's life called BOON, which nobody knows about. It's a malicious portrait of Henry James and they were friends. And you think, 'What's going on there?' James was hugely upset, and the friendship ended. What motivated Wells to so thinly disguise Mr Boon? It's just a straightforward attack. It does happen, but not in my fiction.

Q THE WHITE REVIEW —— Is Peter Scabius an embodiment of the writer's fear of having someone supersede you in terms of success?

A. WILLIAM BOYD —— Gore Vidal famously said, 'Every time a contemporary of mine succeeds a little something inside me dies.' Within the community of writers, we all know what the others are up to and how they're doing. My first novels were published thirty years ago and it's been a long and winding road so for me the challenge is keeping it going. It's not about winning prizes or having films made of your books. It's more about how you ensure as a maturing novelist that your books are still on sale in bookshops and are still being read. I know very eminent novelists who are in their seventies and eighties and you can't buy their books other than in antiquarian bookshops. If you've written twenty-five novels and they're not there anymore, it's hard to cope with. But it's almost an inevitable fate.

The model for Logan Mountstuart was William Gerhardie, the terrifying case study of a very successful young novelist, hugely acclaimed, who wrote his last book in 1942 and died in 1977 – that's thirty-five years of silence and neglect and oblivion. That's the terrifying fear, not how well others are doing.

TRISTAN SUMMERSCALE & JACQUES TESTARD
MARCH 2011

SRI LANKAN CONTEMPORARY ART

BY

JOSEPHINE BREESE

SRI LANKA HAS DEVELOPED A THRIVING, vital contemporary art scene over the past twenty years. New artists are emerging to complement the work of their predecessors, who blazed trails in their employment of novel, often controversial, modes of practice. Yet contemporary art remains firmly outside the mainstream in Sri Lanka, supported by a small percentage of the general public and the efforts of a handful of individuals, universities and galleries.

While the art scenes in Pakistan and Bangladesh are beginning to gain recognition, and Indian contemporary art continues to boom, Sri Lankan art is virtually unknown internationally. The handful of institutions in this country that do promote Sri Lankan work tend to do so in the context of South Asian art, with little focus on the country itself. Not a single Sri Lankan contemporary artwork has ever sold at auction in Great Britain.

With so little attention paid to the scene, the popular impression of Sri Lankan art continues to be defined by the country's most famous movement, the 43 Group. The collective was founded in Colombo in 1943, and sought to pioneer a consciously Sri Lankan interpretation of European Modernism. The 43 Group artists, among them painter Harry Pieris and photographer Lionel Wendt, became renowned for their competitive strain of modernism. They remain the country's most acclaimed artists, despite the group's last formal exhibition being held in 1967.

There followed a period in which Sri Lankan artists began to break with a perceived over-reliance on European Modernism. Prompted by the developments of Abstract Expressionism and the New York School, a seam of abstraction developed. The time was a crucial one in the development of Sri Lankan art, with practitioners moving towards a sustained engagement with their chosen medium.

Sri Lankan art is said to have become 'contemporary' in the early 1990s. The '90s Trend' ushered in a revitalisation of art, characterised by a heightened awareness of the theoretical and conceptual. Sculpture and painting (which continues to be the most popular medium) were now complemented by digital, installation and performance art. There emerged a concerted effort to employ art as a social and political sounding board.

The civil war in northern Sri Lanka had by this time endured for twenty years. The conflict became the subject of explicit political protest in art, standing in stark comparison to the relatively benign themes favoured by the 43 Group. Art was no longer considered a pursuit outside society. Sensitivity to context became a priority, as compulsively communicated through the artwork itself.

While Sri Lankan art was gathering momentum its infrastructure kept pace, and more widely available arts education helped cement this growth. Established figures fostered young talent, recognising the need to nurture future generations and diversify beyond the dominant discourses of the leading voices. The University of

A

Kelaniya was for some time the only institution that offered art to a degree level, but was joined by the Vibhavi Institute of Colombo in 1993. Younger artists converged on Colombo from all over Sri Lanka to learn, and the number of practising artists grew substantially. This in turn saw the theme of urban life infiltrating Sri Lankan art, with the capital city itself becoming a subject.

While it would be reductive to posit a general Sri Lankan 'style' of art, it can be confidently argued that these artists share a commitment to exploring their Sri Lankan background. Sri Lanka is a small island which has experienced enormous upheaval over the last thirty years, which has in turn informed modes of expression and subject matter. Loose categories, which overlap and intertwine, can be suggested for the purposes of this essay.

The first of such loose categories brings together artists that overtly address political concerns. A second would collect those with more abstracted themes and styles, while another group of artists focus on the expression of personal and cultural histories. Associated with each of these groups are some exceptional young artists, whose emergence provides healthy competition for the more established generation.

I.
Vital to any discussion of Sri Lankan art is Jagath Weerasinghe (b. 1954). Weerasinghe has been a significant driving force in the development of Sri Lankan art since the early 1990s, and is presently Director of the Postgraduate Institute of Archaeology at the University of Kelaniya. Weerasinghe coined the phrase '90s Trend', recognising at the time the need for a cohesive framework to describe the activity of his peer group. He co-founded the Theertha International Artists Collective in 2000, which continues to foster new artists and initiatives. He describes current Sri Lankan artists as living in an era of 'para-modernism'.

Weerasinghe's own art, mostly as a painter and draughtsman, is deeply informed by his society's actions. His work reflects an acute political consciousness, stemming from the ethnic riots in 1983 and the actions of the Marxist-Leninist Janatha Vimukkthi Peramuna (People's Liberation Front) government between 1988-1990. Weerasinghe critiques Sri Lankan anxieties, responding to collective attitudes – as he identifies them – and taking themes such as nationhood, ethnicity, religion, identity and violence as his subjects. The artist's work reflects his unresolved tussles with these subjects, as shown by his continued return to themes such as the Dances of Shiva. Dense acrylic and watercolour consume his picture planes in a whirl of feet and legs, stamping out evil in a fury of yellow, orange and black. These intense depictions allow Weerasinghe to explore the troubling contradiction of religious violence and the flaws of institutionalised devotion.

Equally instrumental in the promotion of contemporary Sri Lankan art is

Weerasinghe's friend and contemporary Chandraguptha Thenuwara (b. 1960). Thenuwara is the Director of the Vibhavi Academy, a non-profit art school which he founded as an independent alternative to state-run art institutions. He has stated expressly that he wants his art to influence society through its impact on his audience. His vocabulary constantly regenerates in response to the changing political climate of Sri Lanka, contending that his work is driven by a creative response to 'the destruction that is before us'. In the late 1990s Thenuwara formulated his concept of 'Barrelism', based on the familiar painted metal barrels used by the Sri Lankan military at roadblocks and checkpoints. In Thenuwara's work the objects denote state power and Sinhalese racism. Assuming totemic status, local symbols have become Thenuwara's leitmotifs.

A little younger than Weerasinghe and Thenuwara, Thamotharampillai Shanaathanan (b. 1969) is similarly dedicated to ethical responsibility. Shanaathanan is the most celebrated northern artist and a senior lecturer in art history at the University of Jaffna, the epicentre of the war in Sri Lanka's north. Shanaathanan's work is almost uniquely dedicated to the plight of the Tamil minority. The artist's drawings, prints, paintings and installations have taken on an increasingly dark and disturbing aspect over the last decade. The bold lines of his extraordinary drawings often follow an unknown figure that becomes the subject of the pain that the artist feels in response to the brutal treatment of the Tamil people. Some of Shanaathanan's most poignant work addresses the issue of Tamil displacement.

Maps re-imagined in collage become layered processes of ordering and re-ordering, attending to notions of diaspora. Dispersion from the centre reverberates through Shanaathanan's work. He explores the idea of home, in particular the seeming contradiction of a shared identity and culture in an unfamiliar hostland, with a geographical homeland destroyed by thirty years of civil war.

Shanaathanan was among the Sri Lankan artists to face a new challenge with the end of the war in 2009. In his 'Imag(in)ing Home' exhibition at the Museum of Anthropology in Vancouver in 2010 Shanaathanan approached the power of nostalgia, exploring the importance of memory in forming a collective notion of home.

These three artists are compelled to integrate their convictions about society with their aesthetic preoccupations. This drive is evident too in their shared belief in the power of education. Since the end of the war each artist has conducted a reappraisal of areas of his work. Nevertheless, the end of the war cannot solely resolve their ongoing social critique, which will undoubtedly continue to preoccupy their practice.

II.
The school of artists containing Jagath Ravindra (b. 1963) and Muhanned Cader (b. 1966) can be very broadly defined by their fascination with abstraction. Ravindra's

IV

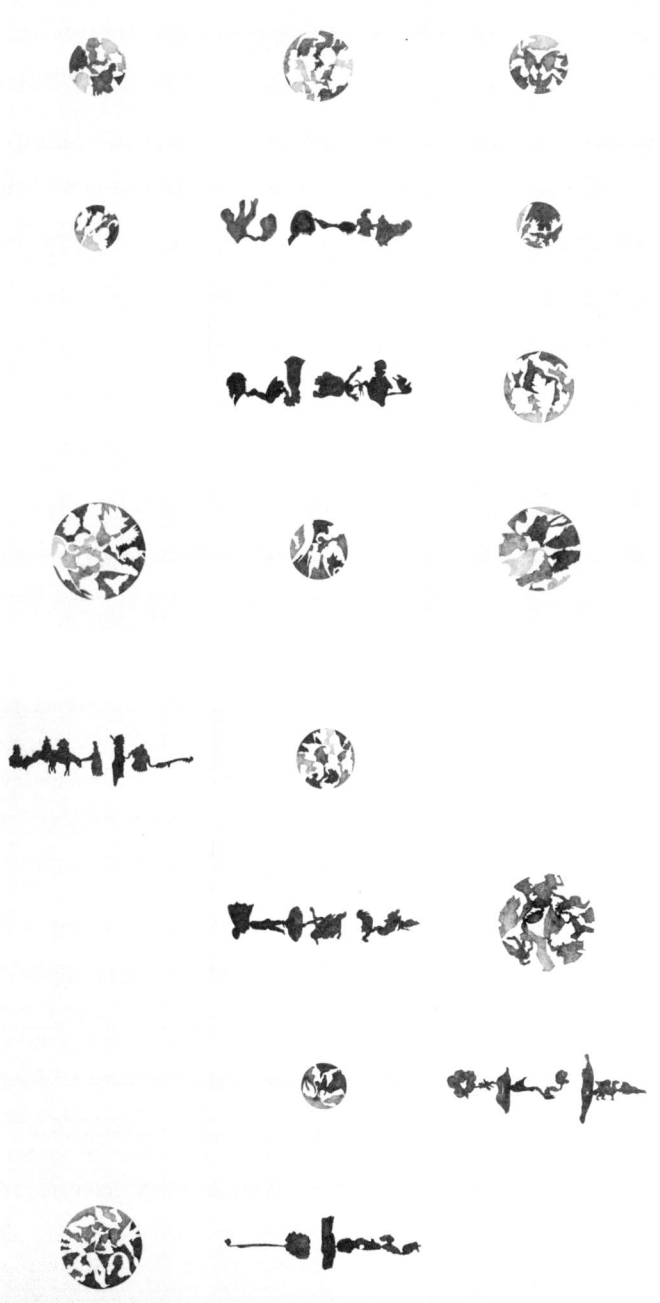

work has been consistently preoccupied with the portrayal of spirituality and the human body. The work does not attend to a specific religion, but is a more universal contemplation of environment. While not as explicitly commenting on the conditions of Buddhism as Weerasinghe, Ravindra's work still responds to the pervasive influence of religion on Sri Lankan culture. His painting is largely abstracted but highly communicative: relationships are established through subtle tonal variation and expressive brushwork, with his use of acrylic paint allowing him to communicate a sense of urgency. Ravindra believes that artists should uphold their responsibilities as citizens above those of being an artist, asserting that one's practice must be examined regularly in order for its message to remain relevant. He is also a prominent figure in the development of art education in Sri Lanka as a lecturer at the University of Kelaniya.

Where Ravindra's technique is expansive and gestural, Cader's methods are strictly ordered and contained. Primarily a draughtsman possessed of extraordinary spatial sensitivity, Cader's work depicts the relationships between images, the subject matter for which has been abstracted from life. His work is often on a small scale, directed by non-linguistic representations of objects and ideas – an imaginative formula of semi-recognisable figures, animals, landscapes and doodles. Cader's audience is presented with 'sentences', joined or separated into spatial cadences and phrasing, the order and narrative of which are left to interpretation. Cader's most recent series, CODED AND LOADED (see *plate* IV), is most advantageously seen in sequence – whether in a conventional linear arrangement or clustered around one another as though in verse. Cader aspires to omit direct political references from his work, but the unorthodox shapes of his canvases and non-rectangular landscapes of his other series can invite political readings. The artist's decision to employ such formats prevents the viewer from seeing the full scene, establishing a visual metaphor for what Cader calls 'true politics'.

A similarly meticulous approach is evident in Sanjeewa Kumara's (b. 1971) work. Veering away from Cader's consistency of method and Ravindra's intense preoccupation with the soaring celestial figure, Kumara heralds an 'art of surprises', with the focus on the surreal and fantastic. An electric palette fuses unlikely combinations and disconnected allusions with a sensual delicacy. Kumara strongly asserts his art as non-Western, rejecting established conventions such as pictorial balance, perspective and spatial depth. While incorporating some Western influences, such as those of pre-Renaissance, 'primitive' artists, Kumara situates his approach away from the Western canon (Weerasinghe has termed Kumara's stance 'Neo-Oriental'). He insists therefore that his works be defined as 'pictures' rather than 'paintings'. Yet thoughtful allusions are contained within his hyper-effusive style. Since the early 2000s Kumara has incorporated political commentary into some of his work, mixing popular and unpopular historical elements alike with visual pastiche.

Setting aside conscious political and religious commentary for the most part, Sri Lanka's cultural history is elegantly handled by Sujeewa Kumari (b. 1971), one of the foremost female contemporary artists. Her work expresses the conviction that Sri Lankans are in a stage of self-discovery, and that history enables a base for growing self-awareness. The female subjects of her paintings wear the (precisely researched) dress of the immediate post-colonial era. Her figures, rendered in close detail, are typically found in abstract, textural settings.

While she does address specifically female concerns, gender issues are not of primary importance to Kumari's work. In contrast, Anoli Perera (b. 1962) works with a vigorously feminist critical voice. Perera is part of Weerasinghe's artistic collective, Theertha, which has run an International Women Artist's Residency for the last decade. The programme was established to promote female Sri Lankan artists, but will end in 2012 having failed to meet its objectives. When female artists graduate there is still a prevailing tendency to return to domestic life. Weerasinghe feels that the challenges inherent in becoming a practising artist in Sri Lanka are not being tackled by women, despite the support offered by the initiative.

III.

A new generation is negotiating the subjects tackled by their predecessors from different perspectives. Dumith Kulasekara (b. 1979) has made a conspicuous entry into the Sri Lankan art scene with two successful solo exhibitions in the last three years, the most recent of which was entitled 'The Symbolical Impossibility of Disavowing Trauma'. Kulasekara's work confronts social and political issues while attending to an acutely subjective excavation of his personal history. The direct influence of Freudian theory is explicit: the artist is his own most revisited subject, closely followed by his wife and mother. Self-portraits range from the more directly representative to symbolic portrayals of the self with abundantly repeated motifs including the floral and phallic. Kulasekara's scenes present surreal mindscapes of heightened colour, incongruous figures, and sensual colour and form, which sit awkwardly against tortured and distended bodies.

Closer to the work of his predecessors, Pala Pothupitiye's (c. 1972) inspiration has undergone a distinct shift in recent years from social and cultural themes of nationality and cultural heritage. Exploring his ancestry as a member of the Sri Lankan dancing caste, Pothupitiye employed and adapted traditional methods of local craft. Thus placing himself within this culture, he also sought to stake out his own identity. The end of the civil war proved to be a moment of profound change for the young artist. The immediate post-war period inspired and troubled Pothupitiye, leading to a solo exhibition at the Saskia Fernando gallery entitled 'Katugaha and

Mythical Landscapes'. The work deals with the idea of 'geopolitical landscapes', addressing the extent to which our understanding of an environment is defined by political considerations.

Shortly prior to this work Pothupitiye produced a series of re-worked survey maps of the island's northern coast. Inlets and islands are transformed into the roaring jaws of a tiger rendered in red ballpoint pen, while headlands become the angry faces of lions, drawn in pencil. Together the lion, Sri Lanka's national symbol, and the tiger, in reference to the rebel Tamil Tigers, form the composite 'liger', a motif which now recurs in Pothupitiye's work.

IV.

The infrastructure of the Sri Lankan art world is slowly expanding to match the artistic developments of the last twenty years. As contemporary art has always had a small audience in Sri Lanka, it has often been presented in tandem with design and architecture. Successful commercial models exist in multifunctional spaces, bringing a restaurant, design and craft element, bookshop and art space under one roof. The Gallery Café, founded by Shanth Fernando, and Barefoot, run by Nazreen Sansoni, followed this model in their efforts to exhibit the best Sri Lankan and international artists. The Saskia Fernando Gallery, established in February 2009, was one of the first independent white cube galleries in Colombo.

Artist-led projects also contribute to the scene. In the absence of more curators and galleries, artists assume multiple roles to encourage the diversity that they envisage for Sri Lankan art. The art collective Theertha was founded with the aim of transcending ethnic and regional borders through artistic connections. In 2007 the Red Dot Gallery was opened by the collective to show innovative art by progressive contemporary artists. Theertha is part of the South Asian Network with India's Khoj International, VASL in Pakistan, Sutra in Nepal and the Britto Arts Trust, based in Bangladesh. Artists often take it upon themselves to curate their own exhibitions. In August 2010 Chandraguptha Thenuwara organised 'Visual Responses During the War', a significant show of twenty-two artists held at both the Lionel Wendt and Harold Pieris Galleries in Colombo. Thenuwara also participated in 'The One Year Drawing Project' with Cader, Shanaathanan and Weerasinghe, a remarkable reciprocal drawing project curated by Sharmini Pereira, and commissioned and published by Raking Leaves, which took place between May 2005 and October 2007.

These different strands collectively represent the support network for Sri Lankan contemporary art. This infrastructure needs nurturing through education and exposure, which will take time. Diversification is vital to the success of the project, and efforts are being made by the University of Jaffna, for instance, to promote artists from the ravaged north. Artists from the south largely recognise and support the development of northern artists.

Contemporary art in Sri Lanka is largely ignored by the general public, and the government makes little effort to change this. Any art that is less commercially viable therefore tends to fall into obscurity, irrespective of its merits on historical, political or aesthetic grounds. Much of the best work is exported or stands in private collections, meaning that the public is denied the opportunity to engage with it. The absence of critical writing is also keenly felt, further obstructing wider recognition for the work. But each of these areas will grow in concert with the others. As elsewhere, a greater diversity is key to healthy development.

Sri Lanka has its own history of modern art, with a formative modernism that paved the way for contemporary art. The past twenty years have seen a revolution in artistic perspectives. Art has become a forum in which to raise difficult issues, whether political, personal or universal. The generosity of older artists with their time and energy has fostered a persistent atmosphere of investigation, exploration and reaction. Sri Lanka's artists are courageous, vocal and prolific. Their work deserves wider exposure and recognition.

For a selection of images please visit thewhitereview.org/art

PORTRAITS OF PIERRE REVERDY

AND

THREE POEMS

(*tr.* SAM GORDON)

THREE PORTRAITS OF PIERRE REVERDY (1889-1960)

ANDRÉ BRETON

The most memorable thing about our meetings [around 1919-1920] was the almost complete bareness of the room in which Reverdy received us, usually on Sundays. He lived at the top of Montmartre, rue Cortot, a stone's throw from the rue des Saules. Of the astonishing 'climate' that prevailed there, nothing could give a clearer picture than this remarkable description by Reverdy himself, at the opening of *LA LUCARNE OVALE*[1]:

> At that time coal had become as precious and as rare as nuggets of gold, and I was writing in an attic where the snow, falling in through cracks in the ceiling, would turn blue.

¶ Such force of expression has for me lost none of its beguiling charm. It takes me back, instantly, to the heart of that verbal wizardry which, for us, was the preserve of Reverdy. Only Aloysius Bertrand and Rimbaud had previously ventured so far down that path. For my part, I loved and I love still – yes, love – this poetry that takes as its subject the vast swathes that halo everyday life, that haze of anxieties and intimations that flutter around our thoughts and actions. From these he pruned as if at random, the rhythm he created appearing to be his sole tool, albeit one that never betrayed him; he was a marvel. Reverdy was much more of a theorist than Apollinaire: he would even have been a master in our eyes had he been less impassioned in debate, more aware of the arguments with which we opposed him, though it is true that this passion made up a great part of his charm. No one has reflected better, nor has known how to make others reflect, on the profound effects of poetry. Nothing could hold greater importance later on than his ideas on poetic imagery. Nor is there anybody who has shown such exemplary indifference to the ingratitude of fate.

(*INTERVIEWS WITH ANDRÉ PARINAUD*, 'Le Point du Jour', Gallimard, 1952)

---

1. Translators note: lit. *THE OVAL SKYLIGHT*. An early volume that first appeared in 1916, and now forms part of *PLUPART DU TEMPS* (Paris: Editions Gallimard, 1998).

LOUIS ARAGON

A BLACK SUN HAS SET IN SOLESMES

When we were 20 (Soupault, Breton, Eluard and I), he embodied for us all that was pure in the world. Our immediate elder, and the exemplary poet. Life may well have ebbed between us, but it has never clouded that image, that dark conscience, that obstinacy, that shadowy voice from our youth. I will not play at measuring this loss – when he was alive I already felt the inscrutable depths of his being... His absence will amplify over the century; what is said today matters little. His greatness – what could I add to it by comparing him to the dead and those surviving? We still have Saint-John Perse and Marie Noël, Apollinaire is no longer, nor Eluard... We take no notice of this unknown man who kept himself to one side, until the sun comes round and his shadow grows, spreading, covering the century.

¶ I can remember him in rue Cortot in that time of destitution and violence, a winter in which there prevailed an extreme, horrific coldness, his wife ill, in the house above that bloody Utrillo who made such a perfect racket – it was utterly dreadful. There was in Reverdy's black eyes a burning fury such as I have never seen anywhere, like charred vine stocks in the dark of night. I remember the day when he had to sell to one of those rich men who so love their art a small Braque – which for him was very much more than a picture – and how at the last minute before he was stripped of it, he had fiercely grabbed the canvas and kissed it with his lips, to the bewilderment of the enlightened connoisseur.

(*Les Lettres Françaises*, 23 June 1960, no. 830)

BRASSAÏ

REVERDY IN HIS LABYRINTH

How to accept that our conversation, begun thirty years ago on rue La Boétie, around the time of *MINOTAURE*, is now forever interrupted; that never again will I happen upon his provincial silhouette, always slightly overdressed, a bit awkward and out of place on the Parisian pavement; that never again will I see his black hat, his gabardine overcoat, his navy blue suit, his bow tie; that never again will I have the pleasure of looking at his unbowed head with its long, thick hair, black like a crow's, sweeping across a stubborn forehead and sitting at the nape of a neck given to abrupt nods of the head, or his tanned, peasant's face ever protruding from a cloud of light silk, his half-opened lips revealing the whitest teeth; that never again will I confront the fire in his eyes, like a little bull, black and squat, ready to charge; that never again will I hear his gravelly and warm 'My dear...', more manly than any voice I have ever known, unforgettable in its resonance.

¶ I met the man before I got to know his poetry. The man shone with health and love of life. His sharp and animated gestures, his voice, his Mediterranean verve, his nervous temperament, his child's laugh, all were those of a man perfectly at ease with himself, who smiled on life and on whom life smiled. He loved to eat and drink, he adored women, the bustle of the street, café terraces, window-dressings, newspapers, books... and he displayed a passionate interest in art and its intimate relationship with poetry. And how he loved to get het up and hot under the collar, whether by an idea that had come to him, or by alcohol, and to lecture or even debate for hours and hours, a man quite at leisure, striding on tirelessly. Nothing in his appearance, in his curiosity always alert to all things, would have led me to believe that this man, so alive, so resplendent and handsome, concealed a wound in his side that he knew to be incurable, as his poetry would later reveal. And I had not yet read his warning, that one must never judge a man on appearances or talk about him without knowing 'what is happening in his head when he finds himself alone, with the light off, under his sheets.'

(*MERCURE DE FRANCE*, January 1962, no. 1181,
special issue *PIERRE REVERDY*, pp. 159-160)

Pierre Reverdy

Main d'œuvre

POÈMES 1913-1949

MERCVRE DE FRANCE
MCMLXXXIX

AUBE SINISTRE
[LE CHANT DES MORTS, 1944-48]

J'ai retrouvé l'île natale
L'archipel des mots libérés
Le sens le plus cruel des gestes furtifs
Dans l'ombre où la crainte se dissimule
Derrière le rideau mouvant de la pensée
A peine le dessein perçant sous les gerçures
Un doigt de miel sur les lèvres ourlées
Le grognement du ciel tard dans les encoignures
Où se cache l'absence d'un amour étoilé
Figure du retour sanglant à main remise
Désastre d'un destin tardivement éclos
Navire fracassé à l'angle des banquises
On joue à qui perd gagne sur les mots
Et sur le sol de sel durci à la lumière
Fatigué de t'entendre écouler tant de pleurs
Fleurs du matin roussi
Cœur dans mes mains de cendre
Dunes mouvantes du désert

SINISTER DAWN
[SONG OF THE DEAD, 1944-48]

I have regained the island
The archipelago of words unbound
The cruelest sense of stolen gestures
In the shadows where fear conceals itself
Behind the twitching curtain of thought
The sketch barely piercing the cracks
A sliver of honey lines pursed lips
The groaning of the evening sky in every corner
Where hides an absence of any starlit love
Turning face bound with hand checked
Disaster of a fate coming late to bloom
Ship shattered at the edge of ice floes
We play word games of loser's chess
And on the salty soil baked solid by the light
Tired of hearing you eke out so many woes
Flowers of the scorched morning
Heart in my hands of ash
The desert's rolling dunes

LE CŒUR TOURNANT
[FERRAILLE, 1937]

Il ne faut pas aller plus loin
Les bijoux sont pris dans la lyre
Les papillons noirs du délire
Remuent sans y penser la cendre du couchant

A peine revenu des voyages amers
Autour des cœurs jetés au fond des devantures
Sur l'avant-scène des prairies et des pâtures
Comme des coquillages nus devant la mer

A peine remué par l'amour de la vie
Des regards qui se nouent aux miens
Des visages sans nom des souvenirs anciens
Diamants de l'amour qui flottent sur la lie

Pour aller chercher au fond dans la vase
Le secret émouvant du sang de mon malheur
Il faut plonger la main aux racines du cœur
Et mes doigts maladroits brisent les bords du vase

Le sang qui jette sur tes yeux ce lourd rideau
L'émotion inconnue qui fait trembler ta lèvre
Et ce froid trop cruel qui emporte ta fièvre
Froisse dans tous les coins le linon de ta peau

Je t'aime sans jamais t'avoir vue que dans l'ombre
Dans la nuit de mon rêve où seul je peux y voir
Je t'aime et tu n'es pas encore sortie du nombre
Forme mystérieuse qui bouge dans le soir

Car ce que j'aime au fond c'est ce qui passe
Une fois seulement sur ce miroir sans tain
Qui déchire mon cœur et meurt à la surface
Du ciel fermé devant mon désir qui s'éteint

P

THE TURNING HEART
[CAST IRON, 1937]

We must not go any further
The jewels are set in the lyre
Delirium's black butterflies
Stir unthinkingly the ashes of the setting sun

Barely back from bitter voyages
Around hearts thrown to the back of windows
Onto the foreground of prairies and pastures
Like naked shells before the sea

Barely roused by love for life
Looks which gather around mine
Nameless faces of times gone by
Diamonds of love floating on the dregs

Looking in the depths of the sludge
For the moving secret in the veins of my misfortune
I must sink a hand into the roots of my heart
And my clumsy fingers shatter the vase's edge

The blood which draws this thick curtain over your eyes
The unknown emotion which makes your lip quiver
And this too cruel cold which drives your fever
Crumples all the corners of the linen of your skin

I love you having seen you only in the shadows
In the darkness of my dream where alone I can see
I love you and you are as yet indistinct
A mysterious form which moves through the evening

For what I love deep down is that which passes
Just once through this two-way mirror
Which tears my heart and dies at the surface
Of the closed sky before my ebbing desire

TEMPS SEC
[SOURCES DU VENT, 1929]

Un feu naturel flambe dans la grille des bois
A la racine prise au fond de la mémoire
Les sentiers imprévus et le ravin plus bas
Le trou creusé du ciel où les bêtes vont boire
Il n'y a qu'un moment plus frais dans la saison
    dont les rousseurs s'effacent
   sur le visage inquiet du vagabond
   toujours conduit et rejeté
   au temps qui le dépasse
La pluie manque au rocher
Le sillon suit son pas
Et l'homme fatigué revient sur la nuit noire
La route de clarté reflète un tourbillon
Une bouffée de mots tièdes qui veulent dire
Tous les oiseaux du ciel cherchent une oraison
Les arbres sont pris de délire
Tout est perdu dans la réalité
   Tout est trop loin pour la main prisonnière
Le filon d'or
  et la lumière
Le dernier regard de l'Été

DRY WEATHER
[SOURCES OF THE WIND, 1929]

A wild flame blazes at the gate of the woods
Rooted down in the depths of memory
Down unknown paths and the gully below
The hole dug in the sky where the beasts go to drink
There is but one fresher moment in the season
              when the freckles fade
        on the anxious face of the wanderer
        always driven away rejected
        by time overwhelming
Rocks long for rain
Furrows long too
And the tired man turns back to the dark night
The lighted way resembles a whirlwind
A gust of warm words which want to speak
All the birds in the sky seek out their prayer
The trees are driven to folly
Everything lost in reality
              Everything too far for the captive hand
Seam of gold
            seam of light
Summer's final glimpse

THE END OF FRANCOPHONIE: THE POLITICS OF FRENCH LITERATURE

BY

LAUREN ELKIN

I.

WE WERE A COUPLE OF MINUTES LATE for the panel we'd hoped to attend. The doors were closed and there was a surly-looking man standing guard next to a sign that read 'Complet' – 'Full'. No more room. A stubby line of six or so people had formed behind him.

'Vous êtes là pour "Je est un autre"?' we asked.

'Yes,' the guard replied.

'Is it really full?'

'Yes,' he said.

'And for members of the press?' I brandished my pass, appealing to the guard's sense of professionalism and media savvy.

'C'est complet.'

My friend Elisabeth and I had travelled from Paris to Brittany to check out the Etonnants Voyageurs (Astonishing Travellers) literary festival in Saint Malo, created by Michel Le Bris in 1990. Every year, around sixty writers converge there to celebrate... well, what exactly we're not sure, but it's got something to do with travel literature, francophone literature, and Russians. In 2009, when I was researching a piece on the French literary milieu, all anyone could talk about was this festival and the movement associated with it: *littérature-monde*.

'French literature is opening outward,' I was told. 'Just look at the success of the Etonnants Voyageurs festival.' This was all the encouragement I needed to book a spot on the TGV to the 2010 edition, which was dedicated to Russian literature, Haitian literature, and the theme of the organisers' new book, JE EST UN AUTRE – I is Other. Of all the literary festivals in France – and there are hundreds – this one is the most political, and the most controversial. This is in part because Le Bris and Jean Rouaud were the major voices behind a 2007 manifesto, 'Pour une *littérature-monde* en français' (Towards a World Literature in French), which ran in LE MONDE and was followed by an anthology of the same title.

Signed by forty-four writers including JMG Le Clézio, Tahar Ben Jelloun, Maryse Condé, Nancy Huston, and Edouard Glissant, the manifesto's argument was twofold: first, that French literature ought not to be divided into 'French' (for work produced by writers born in France) and 'francophone' (read: those writers with origins in France's former colonies) but rather should be considered as one continuous world literature in French. We are witnessing the 'end of *francophonie*', they wrote, 'and the birth of a world literature in French'. Second, they argued that French writers who since the rise of the nouveau roman and post-structuralist theory have been engaged in a 'literature with no other object than itself' should stop navel-gazing and put the world back in the text. Le Bris and Rouaud called for literature 'to rub up against the world to capture its essence, its vital energies', making the *littérature-*

monde movement a sort of randy grandchild of Sartre's *littérature engagée*.

The manifesto's declaration of the 'end of *francophonie*' kicked up quite a fuss in Paris and beyond. No less than two special issues of academic journals were devoted to thinking through the issues it raised. Colloquiums were held in Florida, Denmark, California and New Brunswick. Other responses included a rejoinder in L*E* F*IGARO* from then-presidential candidate Nicolas Sarkozy ('*Francophonie* is not dead!'), and an angry L*E* M*ONDE* article from Abdou Diouf, former president of Senegal and current Secretary of the Organisation Internationale de la Francophonie. But Le Bris and Rouaud were content with their handiwork: the following year, Le Clézio won the Nobel Prize, and when asked if he regretted signing the manifesto he replied that he would do it again.

The manifesto seeks to correct an inequality in the way the French tend to think about francophone literature, one which can be gauged with something I like to think of as the Fnac test. That is: you walk into a French bookshop – the Fnac, La Hune, your local bookseller, whatever – armed with a list of writers: Samuel Beckett, Albert Camus, Nancy Huston, Alain Mabanckou, Marie N'Diaye, Dany Laferrière. Pre-2007, you would find Beckett, Camus, and Huston in the 'littérature française' section, and Mabanckou, N'Diaye, and Laferrière in the 'littérature francophone' section. They all write in French. Camus was born in North Africa, but is considered French, not francophone. Beckett was born in Ireland, Huston in Canada; English is their native language. Both appear in 'French literature' because at a certain moment in their lives they began to write in French. If a writer is white then he can produce 'French literature'. If not – he's 'francophone'.

As far as I know, the Fnac has no official policy about where particular writers should be shelved. But the Fnac test does illustrate an inequality between French and francophone writing that has endured for quite some time, and which the manifesto seeks to address. That such a division should exist seems absurd: you don't hear about English versus anglophone writing. Very often writers from outside the Anglo-American metropolis will be referred to as 'post-colonial' but that term – unstable though it may be – is not used as a hierarchical distinction. No one would argue that Ian McEwan and Salman Rushdie should be placed on different shelves, or that one should be considered English and the other anglophone.

The *littérature-monde* movement works against classifications in general, emphasising the common responsibilities of a shared language. Mabanckou and his colleagues say they have made French their own; it is no longer the language of the coloniser. *Littérature-monde*, according to the manifesto, is a way for 'the French language to become untied from this exclusive pact with the [French] nation' and to become an international poetic language.

This idea has its roots in Goethe's *Weltliteratur*. In an undated essay, Goethe casts world literature as something to work towards, rather than an already existent entity: 'The phenomenon which I call *Weltliteratur* will come about mainly when the disputes within one nation are settled by the opinions and judgements of others'. Goethe had in mind a cosmopolitan community of readers and writers; he envisioned 'a common *Weltliteratur* transcending national boundaries'. Appealing to Goethe would indicate a strong – if unarticulated – desire to heal the politically fragmented francophone world through the salve of the French language. This is essentially the position of Léopold Senghor, who similarly believed in the power of *francophonie* to 'promote a universal humanist model of cooperation between nation-states that was to be realised through the shared medium of the French language.'

Le Bris and Rouaud chose the oft-cited Rimbaldian phrase 'Je est un autre' for the title of their follow-up to the 2007 volume, an anthology published by Gallimard in May 2010 which argues for the empathetic, world-enlarging power of literature. Any novel worth its salt, they claim, enables a 'passage à l'Autre', or 'access to the Other'; writers must learn to live at a 'crossroads of identity' and negotiate the pressure put on them to articulate an 'identité-monde': a 'personal narrative orchestrating this identity'. *JE EST UN AUTRE* emphasises the give and take between writer and world, acknowledging the contrasting influences which combine to create a writer's identity.

Le Bris articulates what he sees as the genius of Rimbaud's statement in terms of travel and exploration: '[The phrase] 'je est un autre' opens the very space of literature – the space, and the mystery, which writers obstinately explore.' Writers set out into 'unknown territory', like 'explorers in a dark forest'; sentences come and go, and guide him, or 'throw [him] off the track'; but when he thinks he is on to something he experiences the 'frisson' of a 'traveller ... with the world crossing through him like a light wind.'

When the festival was founded in 1990, it was to celebrate travel writing. Le Bris told *LIRE* magazine in 1999: 'As a writer, I was suffocating in the French literary milieu, and I needed space to breathe.' He founded Etonnants Voyageurs in the spirit of letting 'the four winds of the world' into French literature. Around that time, Le Bris also founded a magazine of travel writing called *GULLIVER*, largely inspired by Bill Buford's *GRANTA* – which he credits with reinvigorating contemporary English literature. *GULLIVER* gave birth, in 1992, to a manifesto of its own, called *POUR UNE LITTÉRATURE VOYAGEUSE* (Towards a Travelling Literature), the terms of which are remarkably similar, and in some cases identical, to those of the 2007 manifesto. Taking aim even then at the nouveau roman and post-structuralist theory, Le Bris wrote, 'the idea is less to be on the avant-garde and more to be resolutely elsewhere: outside.'

The problem with travel writing, of course, is that it very often confirms an imperialistic relationship between the writer and the lands he visits, implicating the reader in that position. As the critic Charlie Sugnet has written, travel writing too often means a rational, detached, slightly disillusioned writer making a foray out from the centre (usually London or Oxbridge) to the peripheries (Uganda, Benin, Vietnam, Borneo) where he (and it's almost always a he) sees that, as usual, the peripheries are uncivilised, and the people of colour who live there are making a botch of running the place.

Writing about other places and other peoples has proved problematic for ethnographers, anthropologists, journalists, and travel writers (not to mention fiction writers) alike; it is a problem which different disciplines have solved for themselves in different and evolving ways. Perhaps due to a growing awareness of this problem, over the years the festival has become less about travel writing qua travel writing and more about the conjunction of cultures: Etonnants Voyageurs favours foreign writers who write about where they're from, or writers with a sense of hybrid identity, or writers who evoke a strong sense of place in their work. (At most of the panels I attended, it was rare to find a writer who spoke only one language, and frequently they wrote in more than one language.) World literature is now the festival's watchword.

But even if the festival is trying to get beyond the exoticising, Othering tendency of traditional travel writing by inviting writers from those far-off places to speak for themselves, they don't completely avoid typecasting them as cultural emissaries. This may not be the fault of the organisers, but may have to do with the way the French experience and consume culture. The founders' ambition is encyclopaedic. Their zeal for the hybrid and the international is laudable in theory, though in execution it sometimes verges on the absurd. (Russia! Haiti! Je est un autre!) But a festival is not only about the political statements its founders and participants may want to make. It is also about what the audience has come to hear.

II.
If they can even get in to hear it. Being barred from the 'Je est un autre' panel was the first sign that attending the festival was not going to be as easy as getting on a TGV. People started queuing up for panels half an hour ahead of time to go and sit through ninety minutes of book talk in the swelteringly hot seminar rooms. There were a tonne of people milling around, almost none of them under 40. The press attaché told me that something like 60,000 people turned up, coming from all across France, some from as far away as Bordeaux and Toulon. This confirms my burgeoning theory about the performative role culture plays in France – the French will-to-culture that heavily subsidises booksellers even as the actual reading rate decreases. (The will is not always on the side of the masses, but is often imposed on them by the Ministry of Culture, bless its heart.) To the average Frenchman, it is not only important to consume culture but to be seen consuming it. This will-to-culture takes on a particularly moralising component when it comes to other cultures – especially

those formerly colonised by France.

When we finally did manage to get into a panel – 'Géographies africaines' – a lively discussion broke out when the interviewer asked the panellists if they write in order to work against clichés about Africa. Moussa Konaté, a Malian playwright, answered, 'When I moved to France I realised that the French don't know anything about African history, or they aren't told anything about it; they think Africa is all giraffes. We write to say that Africa has a history. It is not all giraffes.'

Florent Couao-Zotti, an author of comic books as well as a recently published detective novel, disagreed: 'I don't think literature is there to work against clichés,' he replied. 'My task is to show reality as I see it.'

Alain Mabanckou, who won the Prix Renaudot in 2006 for his novel MÉMOIRES DE PORC-ÉPIC (Memoirs of a Porcupine), was the most laid-back of the panellists, jaunty in his leather newsboy cap and denim jacket. 'You have to remember that African literature was born precisely at the moment when Africans decided to refuse the clichés that had been drawn of them,' he explained. He recalled the kinds of clichés of Frenchmen he heard growing up in Congo – beret, baguette, handlebar moustache – and the audience roared. 'Literature is made to go against all that.'

'But what sells,' Konaté pointed out, 'are clichés – and the risk is that African writers will fall into the trap of giving editors what they want: misery and clichés.'

'But what constitutes an African writer?' the interviewer asked the panel. Someone mentioned the Haitian/Canadian writer Dany Laferrière's novel I AM A JAPANESE WRITER, which asks, provocatively:

> What is a Japanese writer? Is it someone who lives and writes in Japan? Or someone born in Japan who writes in spite of it? (...) Or someone who isn't born in Japan, who doesn't know the language, but decides one day to become a Japanese writer? That's how it is for me.

Laferrière's novel is a comedy, and his protagonist doesn't get very far as a Japanese writer. But as the novel points out, the relationship between a writer and his nationality can be utterly arbitrary. Of course, in most cases the relationship is far from meaningless, as Laferrière is no doubt aware; if he is being provocative, it is to call into question a literary system in which a writer's work is immediately classified according to where a writer was born. In the post-colonial French context, where a writer is born may or may not form the basis of his classification. Konaté says, 'We call what is written by blacks living in France "African literature" even though all the blacks living in France are not all African. When a black American writes, we don't say it is African literature of America. We say it is American literature. Why in France do we not call it French literature if it's written by those with non-white origins? The day has to come when France recognises this kind of writing not as African literature but as French literature.'

The issue no one raised that might have clarified the difference in writerly identity between a black writer in America and one in France is that French republicanism doesn't allow for any kind of hybrid identity. French republican values, grounded in secularism and universalism, call for the immigrant, or the child of immigrants, to be assimilated into French culture. This insistence on homogeneity means that the writer who was born to Algerian parents and raised in France is called a 'francophone' writer 'of Algerian origin'. Difference sticks out, and undoes the whole picture. A black writer in America may or may not think of himself as African–American, but the category is there. In France, the idea of a hyphenated identity is unfamiliar, which is why the francophone category is at once so useful and so useless. It covers for all manner of non-French identities, but creates an alternative to Frenchness that is not coextensive with being French. One is either French or francophone, but not both. Francophone signifies 'difference', and that category has served the French in this way for quite some time.

III.

To some French journalists, the festival smacks of self-aggrandisement and political correctness. I am reminded of this the next day, at a panel called 'Pour une France plurielle' (For a plural France). One panellist, the actress and screenwriter Ariane Ascaride, described her upbringing in Marseille, where almost half of the city's 800,000 residents are of Italian origin, a quarter are North African, and 10 per cent are Jewish. 'I was born into a mélange of cultures,' Ascaride said, 'and I believe that makes you more sensitive to the immigrant experience.' She kept underscoring the fact that immigrants are welcome in Marseille; why aren't they welcome in the rest of the country? 'I don't understand,' she repeated. 'I don't understand.'

This refusal or inability to think through these problems is something that plagues the French Left as well as the Right. As Konaté had pointed out the day before: 'France is still a victim of her colonial past. People think the colonised are the victims, but the colonisers are as well, somehow. We all suffer from it, from having been colonised, and from having colonised.'

This results in much political posturing about the issue, to the point where the politics seems the main issue, rather than the inequalities the politics ought to address. Le Bris and Rouaud picked up on this in *JE EST UN AUTRE*. 'If France is suffering from its colonial past, it is because its republican universalism finds it impossible to [deal with the consequences],' they write. 'At a moment when we should be celebrating the fiftieth anniversary of the African independences,' Le Bris writes, 'we find a debate around "French identity", which is endlessly self-referential and comes out of a politics of exclusion.' He is referring to the debate about French identity that Nicolas Sarkozy launched in November 2009, asking Eric Besson, the Minister of Immigration (a ministry created by Sarkozy in 2007) to head it up. 'We must reaffirm the values of national identity and pride in being French,' Besson declared. Town hall meetings were held across the country to discuss what it meant to be French and a website was established where people could leave their comments. The site soon devolved into a racist free-for-all: a fifth of the entries had to be deleted.

Sarkozy cast the debate in terms that made him appear sympathetic to the plight of the immigrant in France. 'Am I making up the "ghettoisation" of certain city districts, the rise of a form of racism in others, violence in yet others, the absence of diversity in French elites?' the *INDEPENDENT* quotes him as asking, coyly refusing to acknowledge the role his statements and policies have played in encouraging this kind of racism.

The response to the initiative was derisory; Sarkozy was accused of taking advantage of the tense racial situation in France to win the municipal elections held in March last year. Although in a November 2009 TNS Sofres poll 60 per cent of respondents had said they would be interested in such a debate, while 80 per cent said they felt French identity was 'weakening', a January poll showed that 49 per cent of respondents considered the debate to be essentially focused on Islam, and was largely ignoring issues of French values, culture or patrimony. By early February 2010 Eric Besson announced the debate was at an end, and that new patriotic rules would be implemented: schools must fly French flags (most already do); the 1789 Declaration of the Rights of Man must be displayed in every classroom; students will be given 'Young Citizen's Logs' in which to record their civic activities.

The very fact that such a debate was initiated was a first for the French, who do not keep statistics on immigrants' ethnic background or country of origin, as to mark out a citizen as something other than French, or something in addition to French, would be to violate the republican value that a citizen be seen as French and nothing more. The topic of national (or ethnic) identity is so taboo that only extreme right-wing politicians like Jean-Marie Le Pen would touch it in the past.

The Left was reticent to get involved in a debate on national identity on Sarkozy's terms, and in October 2010 when the National Assembly voted to ban the burqa, the Socialists abstained from voting, thus tacitly allowing the ban, which went into effect last April, to go into effect. 'Why did the Left stay practically mute in this debate about national identity?' Le Bris asks in *JE EST UN AUTRE*. 'The truth hurts: the Left abstained from the debate because its republican model is in crisis, may be at the end of its days, or at least has no longer any grip on reality, but, prisoner of its own mythology, refuses to own up to it.'

What is becoming clear, Le Bris points out, is that French republicanism can be used as a means of discriminating against the not-French. Statistics, he asserts, citing a recent study called *Appel pour une République multiculturelle et postraciale*, are the '"only tool which would allow us to measure the efficacy of public and private policy" ... Today it is the principle of *égalité* which prevents us from putting into action the means to obtain a real equality.' The face of France is changing, and judging from the recent political rise of Marine Le Pen, 15 per cent of the French – who voted for the Front National in the March 2011 local elections – would prefer it remain the same. For the FN, as for Sarkozy, the rhetoric of *égalité* is a tool to enforce the exclusion of the more heterogeneous elements of the population.

Le Bris and Rouaud conceive of the concept of *littérature-monde* as being inclusive in the way that French republicanism is inclusive, leaving unmarked the difference in the writer's origin. If the manifesto calls for a world literature in French, they write, it is because 'judging from all the evidence, there are multiple literatures in the French language throughout the world, forming a vast complex, the ramifications of which link together several continents.' But it seems to me that to group all these writers together would be to ignore the different circumstances which have brought these writers to the French language. It leaves out the very important issue of perspective: the view a writer has on the world, and how it is conditioned by (because where would any conversation be without Bourdieu?) his habitus. But is it terribly Anglo–American of me to insist on a model of visible diversity? Is the 'salad bowl' approach to culture really more desirable than the French ethos of assimilation? Le Bris and Rouaud's solution seems to create more problems than it solves.

IV.

I'm not alone in finding the *littérature-monde* idea untenable: the manifesto has met with no end of criticism in France. Le Bris and Rouaud's way of talking about the 'new energy' that writers from across the world will bring to the French language is reminiscent, as Kathryn Kleppinger has pointed out, of the redemptive role assigned to 'primitive' African art by the Modernists. It seems to assign an impossible authenticity to writers from the periphery, and as Rushdie reminds us in his essay 'Commonwealth Literature Does Not Exist', 'authenticity is the respectable child of old-fashioned exoticism.' Graham Huggan has described this as the 'post-colonial exotic', which 'joins post-colonial literary/cultural production to a naïvely celebratory global sensibility' and can actually end up reifying the imperialist structures ostensibly being opposed. Huggan calls this commodification of marginality the 'alterity industry'.

One problem critics have had with the manifesto is its unclear use of the term 'francophone'. 'How can they announce the end of *francophonie*' the Lebanese writer Alexandre Najjar asked in *Le Monde*, 'when these prizes, which are supposedly such a barometer of contemporary literature, attest to the validity of *francophonie*?' Replacing the term 'francophone' with '*littérature-monde* en français,' Najjar wrote, quoting an old Lebanese proverb, is 'to explain water with water'.

So then why are Le Bris, Rouaud, and the other signatories so anxious to throw out *francophonie*? I sat down with Le Bris on the last day of the festival to talk through some of these issues with him. A former Marxist revolutionary of the *soixante-huitard* variety, he has genuine intellectual street-cred because he spent eight months in prison in 1971 for directing the illegal radical left-wing newspaper LA CAUSE DU PEUPLE (the official organ of the Maoist group La Gauche Prolétarienne). Sartre intervened on his behalf, without success. After his release from prison, Le Bris broke with La Gauche Prolétarienne. Since his activist days, Le Bris has invested his political energy in more legal directions; he has published his own travel narratives and philosophical tracts, and founded a travel literature imprint called Voyageurs-Payot, where he has published writers like Jonathan Raban, Colin Thubron, and Peter Matthiessen (all of whom are regular guests at the festival). We met in the press room on Sunday morning. He looks like a French Jerry Garcia.

'It's not about killing *francophonie*,' he said, 'but rather, it would be better if France could consider itself to be part of *francophonie*. France thinks of *francophonie* as something separate from itself. The French think they diffuse the light of their culture onto the former colonies. We'd rather imagine a space of exchange, within this world-language.' What they aim to do, he told me, is not to throw out the term 'francophone' altogether (on the contrary, they continue to employ it, as do many of the contributors to the anthology), but rather to enlarge the term to include the literature previously known as 'French'.

Alain Mabanckou made this argument in LE MONDE a year before the manifesto was published:

> When we talk about francophone literature, we think quite naturally of a literature made outside of France, most often by writers from the former French colonies. This definition, in its generality, has the merit of cutting short further discussion in order to assuage [French] consciences. And we could apply it to the literatures of all former colonies.

If French literature has been considered one of the '"great literatures" which are supposed to have established the universal model of literary creation,' francophone literature 'is only seen as a literature of the margins, a satellite of French literature'.

At one time, Mabanckou told me at the festival, he thought francophone literature would be integrated into French literature. But over time he began to reassess the relationship between them. It is up to French literature 'to enter into the complex of francophone literature.' If a text is written in French, he says, 'it's a francophone text.'

He elucidated his vision thus: 'To be a francophone writer is to be a depository of cultures, a whirlpool of worlds. To be a francophone writer is to benefit from the heritage of French literature in general, but it is above all to bring a personal touch to a harmonious whole, one that dissolves borders, erases race, reduces the distance between continents in order to achieve a fraternity in both language and the universe,' Mabanckou concluded. 'We will no longer come from a country or a continent, but rather from a language.' Mabanckou's programme does not erase the difference between francophone and *franco-français*. But it is a step towards erasing the hierarchy which exists between them.

Until France can come to terms with difference, until France can find a new version of its republican model that allows for hybrid identities, until France can find a way to consider multiculturalism not as inherently bad or inherently good, but rather as a fact of twenty-first century geopolitical life, this hierarchy will persist. The *littérature-monde* movement emphasises the common responsibilities of a shared language, but only hints at the question of how these responsibilities are inflected by the particular relationship between France and its former colonies. These 'erasures' seem to pose a significant, unresolved (and perhaps irresolvable) problem. How much do we want to erase when we are assimilated into a culture, and how much ought to remain? These are questions that go beyond France's borders.

While it may be true that the *littérature-monde* manifesto is somewhat undercooked, at least it is trying to negotiate this problem in the context of post-colonial France. The central argument of JE EST UN AUTRE brings the I and the Other together in a joint alienation – no one is familiar, not the Other and not the Self. 'If there is a "secret" to travelling (and to literature),' Le Bris writes, 'if there is something at play in the fluid space of wandering, it is perhaps this: the point of reversibility between the Same and the Other, the interior and the exterior, that is so difficult for us to think through, but which we feel so violently.'

FROM BACK HOME

BY

JH ENGSTRÖM

MEMORIES MOULD OUR MIND. Lodged inside us they shape the way we are, grounding us in the past and structuring our interpretation of the present. In his collection FROM BACK HOME the Swedish photographer JH Engström traced his childhood memories back to the province of Värmland, in the west of Sweden. Together with his friend, the internationally acclaimed photographer Anders Petersen, Engström revisited his native land to pay tribute to the people, light and landscapes.

Having worked for two years as an assistant to Mario Testino in Paris, Engström moved back to Sweden in 1993, when he started to collaborate with Petersen. After completing his studies in Film and Photography at Gothenburg University and publishing his first book, SHELTER, he moved to New York. He was shortlisted for the Deutsche Börse Prize in 2005 for his book TRYING TO DANCE, and has exhibited in galleries across the world. He now lives and works between Värmland and Paris.

FROM BACK HOME (Max Ström, 2009) was awarded the book prize at Les Rencontres d'Arles and comprises a multifarious collection of coloured and black and white portraits, landscapes, still-lives, close-ups and aerial shots. The images are united by a sense of spontaneity, an ephemeral tone that lends them an air of tenderness. These are works of intimacy and loss, exploring questions of time, memory and the possibility of return. THE WHITE REVIEW talked to Engström about his practice, and about the selection of photographs here published.

Q. THE WHITE REVIEW — What was it that prompted you to return to Värmland in 2001? The lakes, light, landscape... ?

A. JH ENGSTRÖM — Yes all of those things, and the simple fact that I wanted to get away from cities for some time. The contrast between big cities and nature is a theme which has preoccupied me in my life and in my photography. I also became the father of twins and remembered the freedom I felt in nature as a little kid.

Q. THE WHITE REVIEW — Were you afraid of distorting your childhood memories?

A. JH ENGSTRÖM — No, I never had any of those fears. I don't believe you can control your memories. Of course things had changed, because I had changed.

Q. THE WHITE REVIEW — Your projects tend to stretch out over a number of years. FROM BACK HOME is a collection of photographs taken between 2001 and 2008. Did your work change over that period?

A. JH ENGSTRÖM — With the FROM BACK HOME project everything came very easily to me. Going back just triggered these deep emotions and brought them back to life. It affected my work in the sense that it confirmed my belief that if you stop thinking about your role as a 'photographer' or 'artist' you will inevitably come nearer to a kind of honest expression.

Q. THE WHITE REVIEW — It feels as if a shorter period of time would have failed to do justice to the subject.

A. JH ENGSTRÖM — I'm glad you read it this way. I believe that time is among the most important tools in my work. Honesty is slippery, but time helps you to approach it.

Q. THE WHITE REVIEW — You question whether

it is ever really possible to 'go back home'. What does home mean to you?

A. JH ENGSTRÖM —— I still don't know what home means to me. Maybe it is the place where you feel the least restless. The question is one that is constantly present in my work. But I don't think photography takes me back to anything. I believe, or hope, on the contrary that it takes me forward, even if it always, per definition, deals with the past. The idea of what memory is interests me, though. Perhaps it is an altogether abstract universe. In any case, I have strong doubts as to whether it is even possible to translate memory into language.

Q. THE WHITE REVIEW —— Do you always carry a camera?

A. JH ENGSTRÖM —— I have it with me most of the time. But I use all sorts of different kinds of formats. In other words, I don't always carry around my 4×5" on a tripod!

Q. THE WHITE REVIEW —— You have a very eclectic visual language. Many of your images have a particularly oneiric quality (I'm thinking in particular of your smoggy faded images). What is it about the medium of photography that appeals to you the most?

A. JH ENGSTRÖM —— Its directness.

Q. THE WHITE REVIEW —— A few years ago you said 'I'm always looking for presence. Whenever I try, my doubts get unmasked. Easier then to stick with absence.' This statement has been frequently requoted. Does it still ring true for you today?

A. JH ENGSTRÖM —— Yes it does. All the questions built into that sentence are also reasons that photography appeals to me. Presence goes beyond any language. Maybe that's why we keep on trying to capture it.

Q. THE WHITE REVIEW —— The stillness, the clarity of colours and simplicity of the landscape adds an element of melancholy to your portraits of the Swedish countryside.

A. JH ENGSTRÖM —— For me it's very simple: the landscape is there and I recognise it. I also like it. Maybe the melancholy comes from the fact that Sweden has four very distinct seasons. This makes the notion of time passing very present, and perhaps this transience is closely connected to melancholy.

Q. THE WHITE REVIEW —— There is a similar feeling of nostalgia and emptiness in many of your photographs. How does this connect with your idea of the impossibility of going back home?

A. JH ENGSTRÖM —— Well, as I mentioned before, photography is by definition connected to the past. But this doesn't necessarily mean it's 'about' the past. I'm not sure that it's actually impossible to go home. But it's going back home that's impossible. Indeed, some people claim they've found their home, so I guess we have to believe them! But then again, others never really come home. And of course, there is also the notion of an inner homecoming...

Q. THE WHITE REVIEW —— Your book *From Back Home* was produced in collaboration with Anders Petersen. How has your friendship and partnership with Petersen influenced your work?

A. JH ENGSTRÖM —— He has been and still is the person who has taught me the importance of hard work. His obsession about expressing himself has also always inspired me greatly. Moreover, he has always been incredibly supportive of what I try to do.

Q. THE WHITE REVIEW —— You lived in Paris when you were very young. How did this affect your relationship with, and perception of, Sweden?

A. JH ENGSTRÖM —— It made me reflect more on Sweden. It gave me another perspective and enabled my view of Sweden to become less obvious and more critical. This applies to my relationship with Paris too. I had an outside/inside outlook. I like those dynamics.

Q. THE WHITE REVIEW —— At the moment you're working on your upcoming book, the final part of your trilogy [which also comprises TRYING TO DANCE and HAUNTS]. What will you be focusing on this time?

A. JH ENGSTRÖM —— The focus is a love story, a pregnancy and a birth.

Q. THE WHITE REVIEW —— Just to end, there's a beautiful passage by Maurice Blanchot, which came to mind after looking at your work and which I thought you would enjoy. 'The essence of the image is to be altogether outside, without intimacy, and yet more inaccessible and mysterious than the thought of the innermost being; without signification, yet summoning up the depth of any possible meaning; unrevealed yet manifest, having that absence-as-presence which constitutes the lure and the fascination of the Sirens.'

A. JH ENGSTRÖM —— I like that quote a lot.

EUGENIA LAPTEVA

FEBRUARY 2011

I

VI

VII

VIII

IX

x

XI

XII

II

XIII

XIV

XV

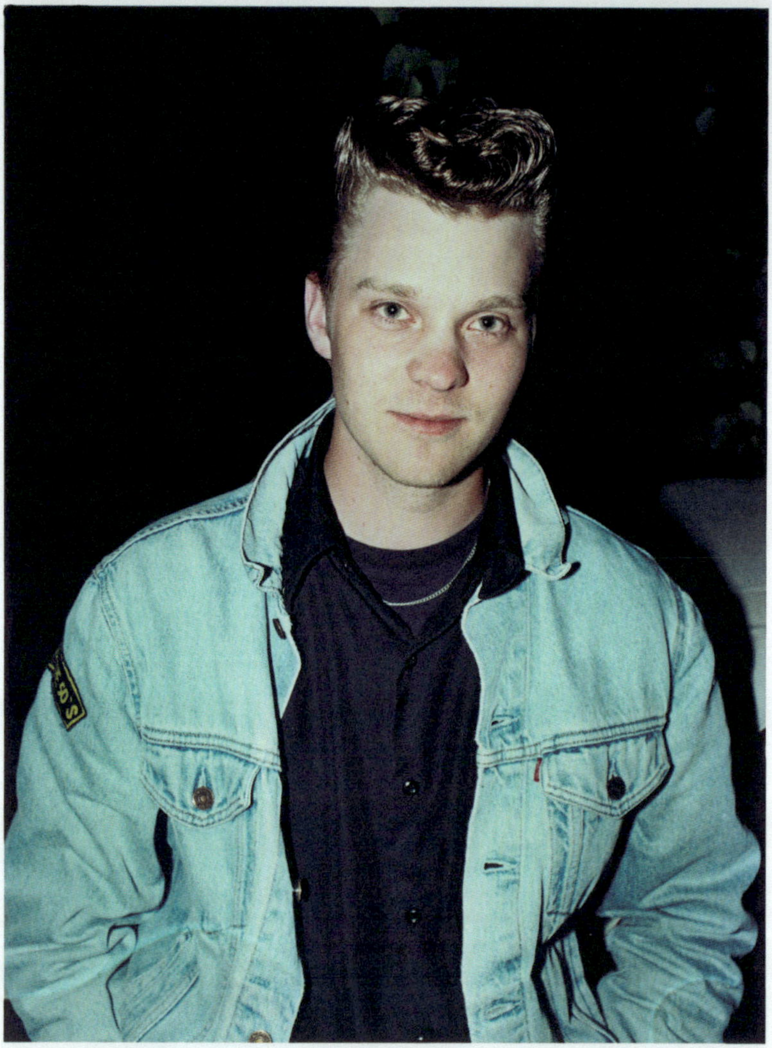

XVI

XVII

XVIII, XIX, XX, XXI

III

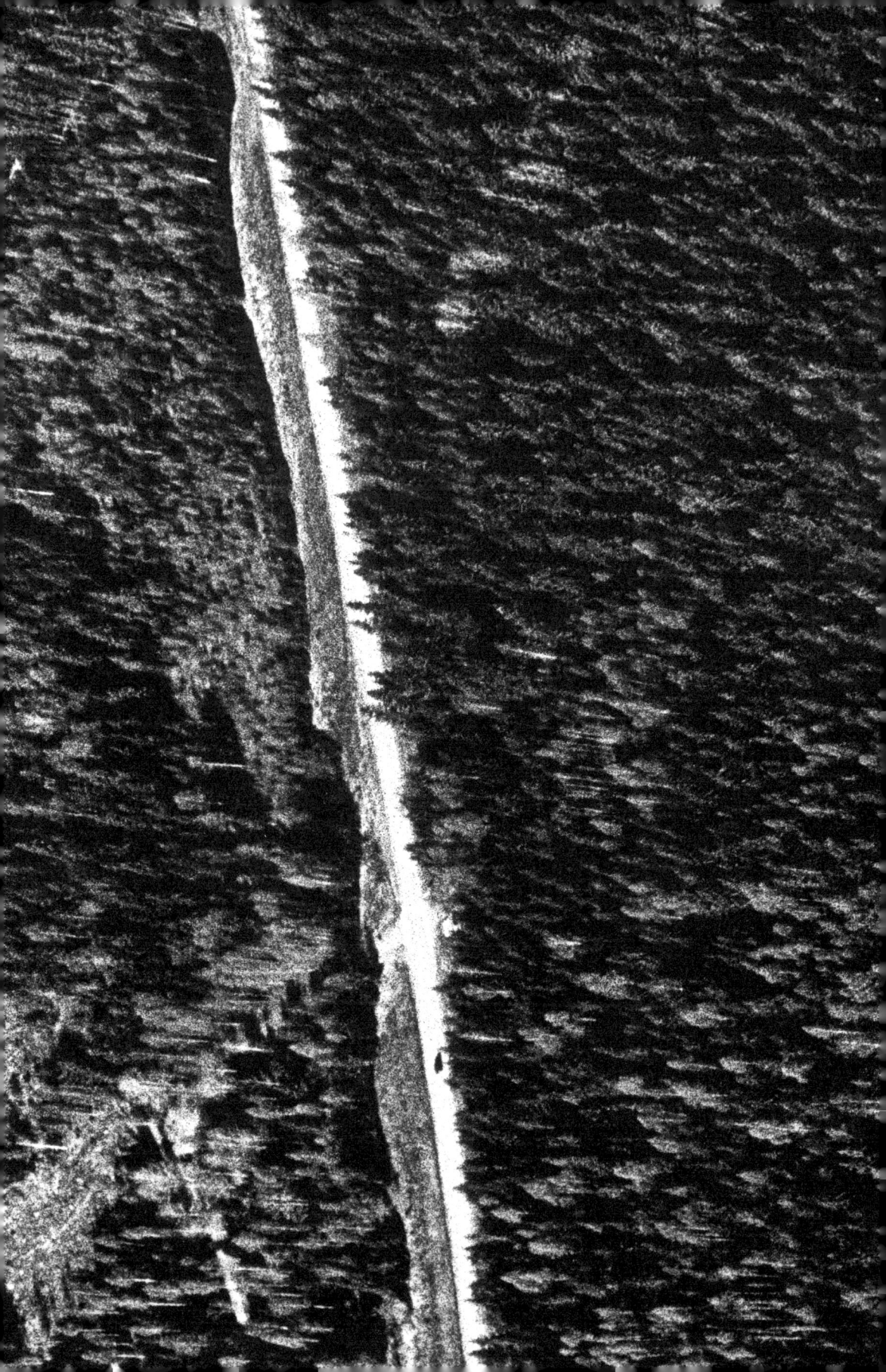

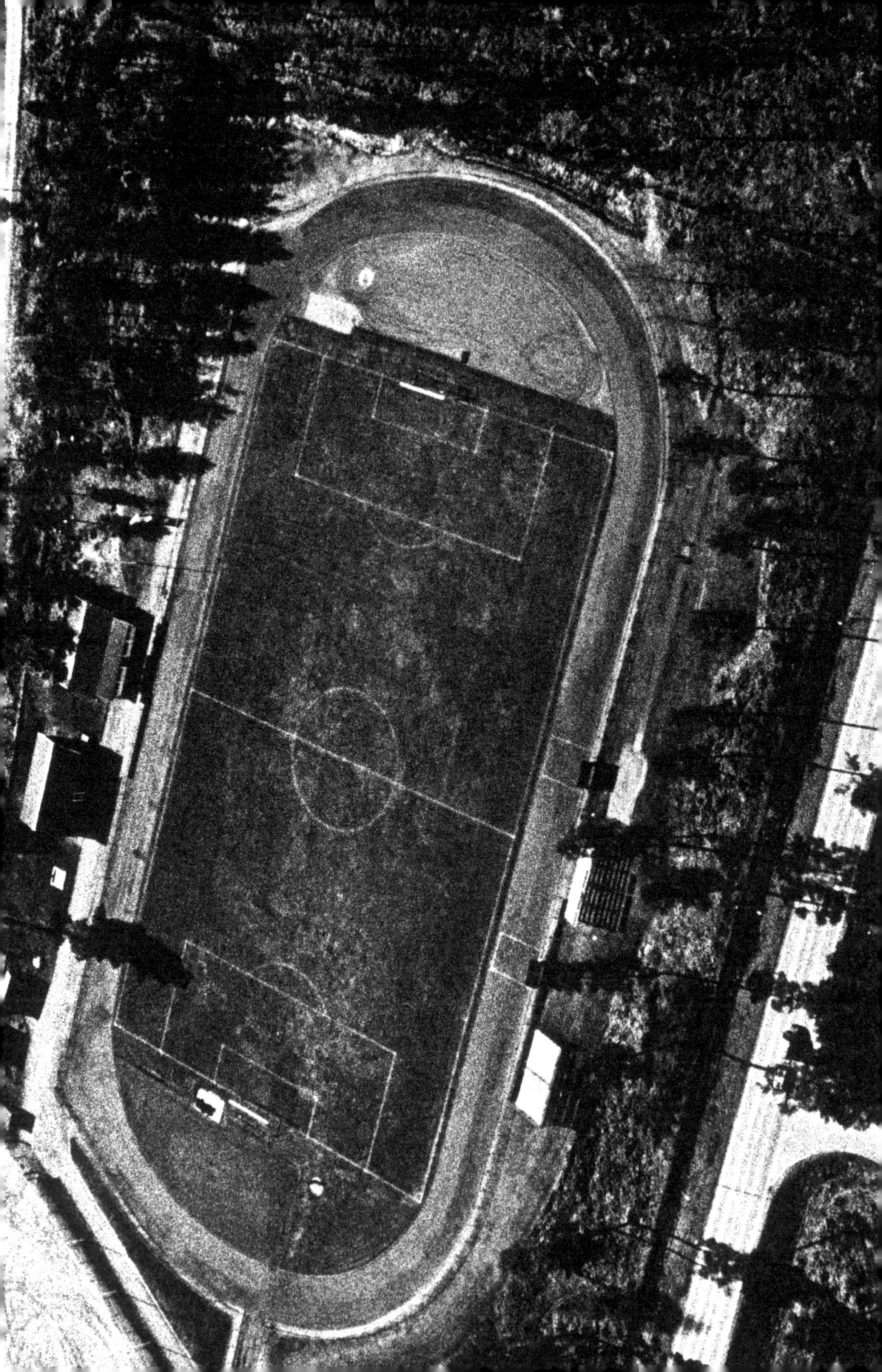

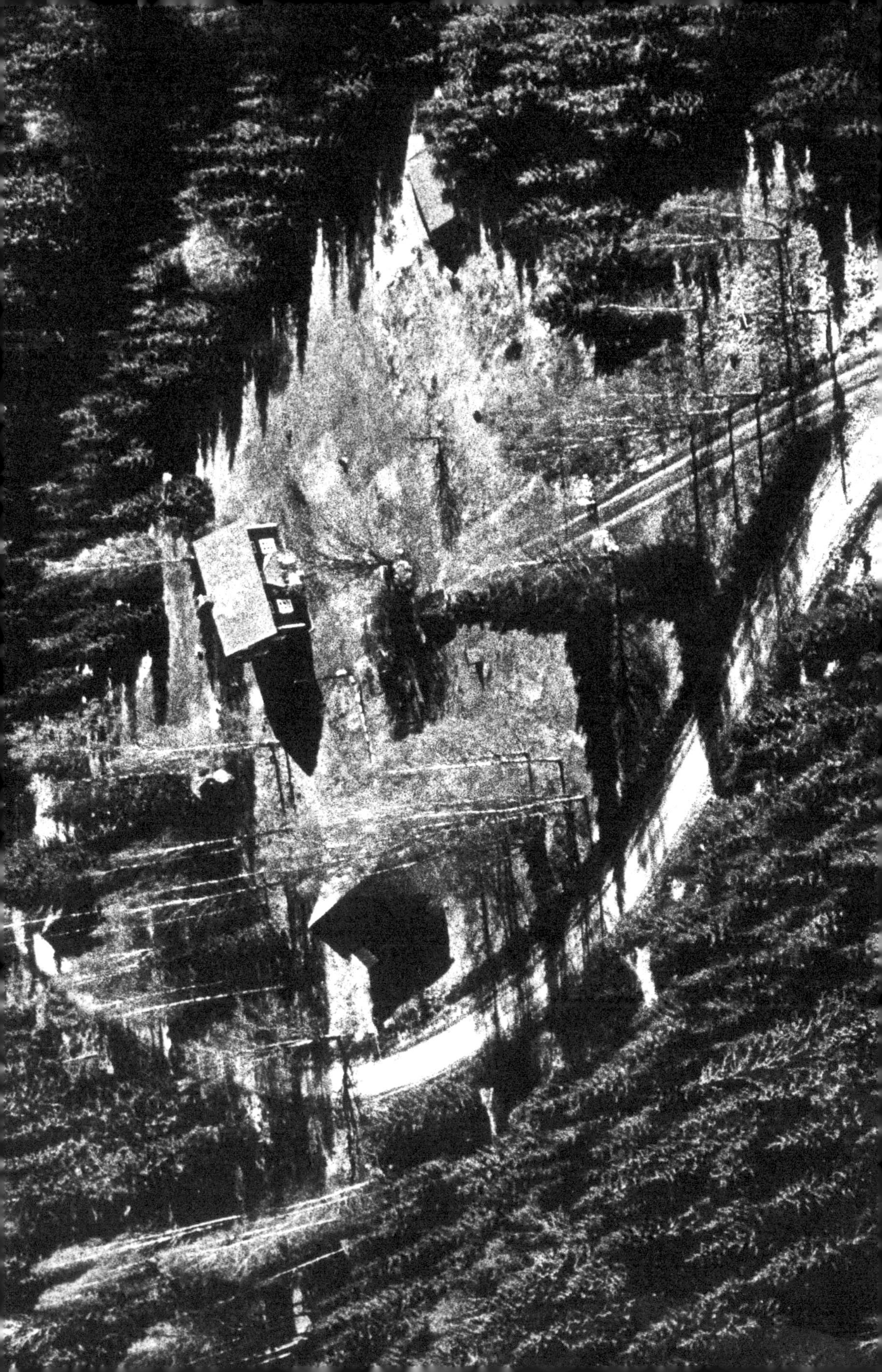

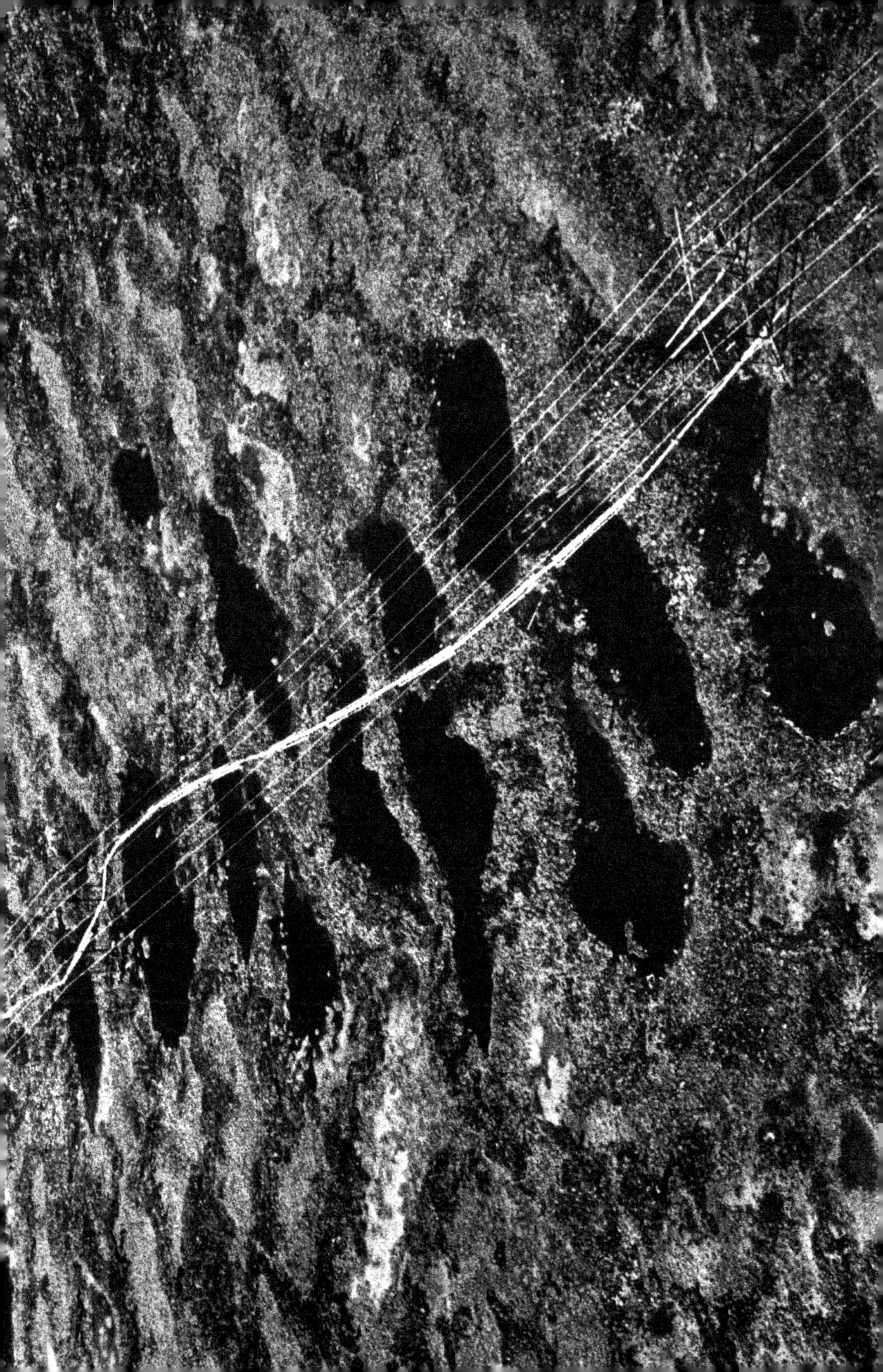

INTERVIEW

WITH

RICHARD WENTWORTH

RICHARD WENTWORTH IS AMONG THE MOST INFLUENTIAL ARTISTS ALIVE IN BRITAIN. He emerged in the 1970s as part of the loosely grouped New British Sculpture movement, defined by their collective reaction against the predominantly po-faced austerity of Minimalist and Conceptual art. Wentworth's sculpture takes as its subject the semantics of the everyday world, taking readymade and frequently incongruous objects and arranging them in a fashion that forces us to recognise the drama inherent in that which we too easily dismiss as routine. His photography captures the unusual or counter-intuitive behaviour of things, treating the (generally urban) landscape as consisting of readymade works that merit the same attention as more traditional art objects. The effect might be compared to having a film of dirt removed from one's eyes: it is often said by his students that, after talking to him, one begins to 'see the world as a Wentworth', meaning that one suddenly has a heightened awareness of the position of objects in one's environment, and a refreshed curiosity in how they came to be there and how we might interpret them.

Wentworth is an enormously charming companion, his conversation characterised by a deft sense of humour, the lightness with which he carries his evident intelligence, and a whirling, associative means of answering a question. Thoughts and ideas are energetically chased rather than followed, the whole exercise being more reminiscent of pursuing a fox possessed of bountiful and very advantageous local knowledge through a series of prickled bushes, many-specied undergrowths and unaccommodating tight-spots than the more stately process described by the traditional metaphor of travelling behind a train. The effect being, of course, that both the journey and the final destination are infinitely less predictable and more exciting. Between 1971 and 1987 Wentworth taught at Goldsmiths' College, London, and has been described, along with Michael Craig-Martin, as a 'godfather' to the Young British Artists (YBAs) that emerged from under his tutelage in the late 1980s. In 2002 he was made Master of the Ruskin School of Drawing and Fine Art at Oxford University, and also tutors at the Royal College of Art, London. With his determination to rework and glorify the everyday, his evident distaste for the notion of the artist as hero or redeemer, and his sincere belief that what surrounds us is as fascinating as that which we feel obliged to gawp at in a gallery, he influenced a whole generation, and continues to influence a new one.

Q. THE WHITE REVIEW — You've said of your son that he's 'smart like an artist is smart'. What makes an artist smart?

A. RICHARD WENTWORTH — I said that of my son because he went to Oxford but he found that he wasn't suited to the course. He found himself on a high maths course. He'd thought it was an engineering course. And he's very very smart but he's smart like artists are smart. He's not an artist but he has that kind of observational intelligence possessed of artists which is a nice thing, but it's not an academic intelligence, or often isn't.

Q. THE WHITE REVIEW — How is this observational intelligence distinct from academic intelligence? Is it related to thinking in images?

A. RICHARD WENTWORTH — It might be, I don't know. It might be that some people are travelling in images in some immensely elaborate way, in the sense that all images are translated. But I still have no idea what an image is, I think it's amazing, and I've even less idea of what makes an image successful. For instance, I just spent an afternoon looking at 6,000 images of artworks for an open exhibition and I don't suppose more than five did *that* [snaps fingers]. It doesn't mean it was all bad work but there's something very odd about the way that some can just trigger an *alert*. I'm very interested in whether people think through text, or how they use text. I'm not a good reader, for instance. I seldom read a whole book. I read parts of lots of books. That's obviously some procedural fault in me, something to do with impatience or wanting to pick things out of the cake. I now realise that's something I was living with when I was a child. But I don't come from an intellectually engaged family.

Q. THE WHITE REVIEW — What's the process of translating images? Who does the translation? Is it a cultural thing?

A. RICHARD WENTWORTH — Well it has to be a cultural thing. Saying that, when I meet people I know almost at once whether there is a mutual kind of engagement, whether we interpret things the same way. And it would upset me to think that this is merely a tribal thing, dependent on having a shared education or cultural space. It's necessarily about being restricted to the same cultural confines – but when you meet those people you don't have to do much translation. There are two or three people with whom I exchange photographs on an arbitrary basis – I send them something, they send me something and we don't need to say anything else, we don't write anything to accompany the photo. That's something of what an image is – it has to have a component which is unaccountable, which sweeps over you. That seems to be beyond translation.

Q. THE WHITE REVIEW — So the image should actively resist translation?

A. RICHARD WENTWORTH — Well it's an art school cliché that bad work is illustrative. What makes things incredibly difficult is the shocking fact that we're all literate. It's very difficult to find anyone who is in a technical sense illiterate. So we're always translating things. It's very difficult to imagine, psychologically, what it would be like to *not* translate everything. If there was a sign over there that said 't-o-i-l-e-t' I would have registered its meaning without really looking at the letters. Something about the transferrable and legible is very hard to delve into.

Q. THE WHITE REVIEW — Do you think that our collective literacy, and the amount of time we spend with words, means that we're inclined to reduce images to words? We unconsciously ascribe meaning to things without actually looking at them?

A. RICHARD WENTWORTH — Well I think that's what reading *is*. I suppose when you're really alert to this is when you're with an under-five. When I was at school, I remember being hit for not forming letters properly – I remember having a 'd' and 'b' crisis, not being able to remember which was which. My son was very dyslexic, and for a long period he would point at the sign above the Jobcentre and say 'That's my name.' And we'd say 'No! You're called *Joe*!' And of course all the fundamental energy of recognition was at work, however that's organised. And if you think about it, the difference between those two words, in terms of the image, is tiny – two small semicircles.

Q. THE WHITE REVIEW — But now we can't stop ourselves 'reading' everything?

A. RICHARD WENTWORTH — I become more and more interested in organisational imagery, which is a kind of text. Everything can be read. Floorboards can be 'read'. The fact that you're sitting comfortably in this room suggests that you've 'read' from the surroundings that the ceiling is unlikely to cave in. A lot of these things you can test by reversing them, by finding those times when you read things wrong. You can become alert to misperception. You have to work hard at it though because the whole point of misperception is that you correct it. So, just as you start to trip or misjudge the height of a step, you correct yourself. What I've enjoyed doing is trying to collect up those moments, those milliseconds.

Q. THE WHITE REVIEW —— Is it then about counteracting the automatism of the way we perceive the world?

A. RICHARD WENTWORTH —— You try and interfere with your own robotic actions, I suppose. One of the things that's interesting when you send a child out to get something in an urban situation, when you ask a child to engage in first basic life tasks, is that a child is in fact so animalesque that it won't actually walk in front of a lorry to see what happens, even though it may never have encountered one before. That's a huge part of how we are, that instinct, but it's set against another force, which is curiosity. So I watched that same son put his fingers into a power socket to see what happened while I watched from a ladder. And I couldn't find the language to tell him to stop quickly enough. He got his first electric shock aged nineteen months or whatever. But he's that sort of guy. How we know what to be curious about and what not to be curious about fascinates me. There are many things we are curious about that we shouldn't be...

Q. THE WHITE REVIEW —— Fire?

A. RICHARD WENTWORTH —— Well I've actually had little arguments with Marina Warner after saying that men are more interested in fire than women. She's offered to come and do something at the RCA on the subject of risk. Curiosity is related to risk. Risk is important. I think that testing to the point of breaking is important. I'm from the generation that could be said now to have taken lots of sexual risks. And you're from the generation that has internalised all these lists of reasons to maybe not, like health and safety assessments. So there's a generational difference in attitudes to risk. But risk occupies a speculative space. Artists are on the whole like that.

Q. THE WHITE REVIEW —— It's interesting to hear you talk about the speculative because your work is very precise in its assembly of objects, it's very meticulous. Yet there remains that sense of precariousness, of the possibility, even likelihood, of failure. Is that part of this boundary space, this arena of speculation and risk?

A. RICHARD WENTWORTH —— Failure is the right word, yes, or the possibility of it. I need to learn more about the quattrocento word 'disegno', which doesn't translate as 'design' but is obviously related. Instead it covers the whole realm of organisational intelligence that humans have. For instance, out of a kind of unsureness about what to do I'm eating from a tray. You were given a saucer and I wasn't. And I remember thinking: 'Do I mind?' And you know a saucer is a classic art object — it's a base, it's an arena, it's a performance space. It's the basis of Cézanne and Picasso. Incredibly well built-up organisational protocols exist to control these variables. And I think that when I put something into the world I'm negotiating with those protocols, but not in a 'design' way. But people mistake that, there's a critical group who think that it's much more deliberate.

Q. THE WHITE REVIEW — Is that about the agency or authority of the artist? Because the more traditional understanding of the artist's role is that he or she determines composition, that the artist plays God and is by nature infallible. But you seem to be giving greater independence to the objects. This suggests you can be wrong.

A. RICHARD WENTWORTH — Well it's not animism, but it is to do with giving some of that agency back. I read somewhere recently, I can't remember where, that there is a branch of physics, a space between science and philosophy, in which people are arguing that, for example, these packets of sugar are in a physical sense having a 'conversation'. It's absolutely typical that I don't have a hold of that. I remember reading it and thinking 'that's very close to what I think.' I derived a sense of companionship from it, a reassurance that I'm not an idiot. But what I do is not theorised. It's not coming out of a set of highly codified elements which I've worked out how to lock together. And that fear — that fearfulness, a nice biblical thing — is actually what enables me to function as an artist. It also prevents me really from being any good as a studio artist. I find that production process like a *petite mort*.

Q. THE WHITE REVIEW — Can you expand on this idea of fearfulness? Is it an anxiety?

A. RICHARD WENTWORTH — The absolutely fundamental anxiety is the classic artist's anxiety: 'Am I any good?' But it's typical of an artist to say that in an interview. It's presumptuous to say that anxiety is the artist's prerogative. I think it's fucking tough to be a human. Mostly we don't know what the point of our existence is and spend the majority of our cheesy little lives trying to invent some inter-nalised meaning beyond survivalism, beyond avoiding the truck when we cross the road.

Q. THE WHITE REVIEW — So we have to invent frameworks of meaning and impose them on the world?

A. RICHARD WENTWORTH — Well I think it's about how you scope the world. I'm quite interested in the image of a handrail. You don't need it but it's good to have it there for when you trip. Part of civilised intelligence is to have noticed that it existed before you trip, not to be looking around for it mid-fall. I'm coming to the age now where I see people ten years older than me using the handrail and I find it horrifying. There's a crossing over there between the metaphorical and the simple biological fact of our spatial intelligence.

Q. THE WHITE REVIEW — This idea of recog-nising one's spatial environment without necessarily registering it consciously is a biological thing, no?

A. RICHARD WENTWORTH — Yes, well it happened to me at the bus stop actually. I was fiddling with my phone and I took a step back and found, to my horror, that the bus stop against which I wanted to lean wasn't where it was when I had arrived. Someone had come into that space between me and the back of the bus stop, because it was raining, and I trod on their toe. A minor social thing ensued. What engaged me about the incident was that I hadn't figured that change. It's interesting that I'd moved into the bus stop and recorded the distance between myself and the back of the bus stop, and later relied on that stored information without considering it. That knowledge of where things are in relation to you is a spatial intelligence. In a way that's very like vocabulary. It's like the moment of risking a new word when you're young. That age between 15 and 20 is so self-conscious — you can be determined to shoehorn the word 'ambivalent' into a sentence because you've recently learned it, and often you make a fool of yourself doing it. If you're lucky you're around other people doing it too, because that creates a cultural space in which that kind of behaviour is acceptable. There's a collective pleasure in trying stuff, with the ultimate aim of learning to inhabit the world. Words are tools to that end. Conversation is a miraculous thing. It's extraordinary that we can meet and talk.

Q. THE WHITE REVIEW — It's interesting that you conceive of language in spatial terms: you talk about language as an 'awareness' of things, an environment almost. And there are gaps and spaces in it.

A. RICHARD WENTWORTH — In every form there's a sense of inadequacy. It's why I talk so much, because I have a profound sense that it's all wrong. It's nearly neurotic, a kind of overcompensation. Dorothy Cross has said that the two of us 'suffer from gregariousness'. Which is needy in some way, there's no other reason I'd spend time working with young artists. Fuck knows why I need that but I do. It's rewarding, for me at least. It's a very privileged position, to be part of the work of a new generation. I can't start wearing leather jackets again but you know it's nice to be there. There's something there to do with imprecision. You know I spend quite a lot of time in etymological dictionaries. I did Greek and Latin, but I was such an unhappy schoolboy I fucked up my Greek, hopelessly, and I really regret it because I think it's a great privilege to have those languages. It's like having extra keys. And a lot of this is tied up with being English, or speaking English at least. It makes you spectacularly hybrid. Every time you form a sentence you're dashing around Europe. It is phenomenally *juicy*, it's like a toolkit. I don't believe anyone ever told

me that though. I've spent time around people whose work is words and I've always felt like the idiot. I don't think I'm without intelligence, but I think I'm somehow criminally smart.

Q. THE WHITE REVIEW — Criminal? In the sense of stealing ideas?

A. RICHARD WENTWORTH — There is something of that. I am quite light-fingered I suppose. I'm very acquisitive, but I'm not a shopper.

Q. THE WHITE REVIEW — So you come across things by accident? And then take possession of them?

A. RICHARD WENTWORTH — I need to believe it's by accident, although what accident is, or whether there really is such a thing, I couldn't say. I am nosy though.

Q. THE WHITE REVIEW — There seems to be a conscious effort in your work to remind us of the processes by which we think, to reinvestigate the everyday. When we see a stop sign we stop, we don't consider the word and then stop. But in your work, your photography particularly, I see an impulse to reconsider these things?

A. RICHARD WENTWORTH — Well yes. Look at this handrail. This handrail could be considered a weapon, but because of the context we don't consider it as such.

Q. THE WHITE REVIEW — This seems to bind in with your approach to etymology — a means of reminding ourselves that words have a narrative rather than a fixed meaning. So meaning is contingent?

A. RICHARD WENTWORTH — Contingency is exactly the right word. I like the contingent. I hadn't thought of it before but the etymology of contingent includes the word 'touch' [Latin 'contingere': to touch]. Its something to do with that idea of contact, that friction, that I really love. Years and years ago I remember getting my first copy of Partridge's ORIGINS — I think I have five copies now, I have one wherever I spend time — and I remember finding out that 'cornea' and 'corner' and 'horn' share a root. That's just amazing. I'm interested too in monograms, though not very knowledgeable. You don't see them very often now but I think they're rather extraordinary. At the end of the nineteenth century they were popular — you can see one in King's Cross — KXL for King's Cross Laundry. It's arts and crafts. It's very beautiful. All the crafts available at the time are employed in the manufacture of this monogram — there are a series of forged monograms in the metal fence, one built into the stonework. There are these different languages. This was a high point of that language. That's very much like what a good etymology is like. It's like a rebus. Like a knot.

Q. THE WHITE REVIEW — Do you think of constructed ideas or objects as knots? You know, people always talk of your work as a putting together of incongruous objects, but it's always seemed to me to have more to do with pulling things apart. You're presented with something and you want to break it down?

A. RICHARD WENTWORTH — Well I'm interested in the way things are constructed. I'm from the end of that period in which people were good with their hands. If you were nicely brought up it was considered slightly odd to be interested in these things. In fact, I'm only really one notch away from the 'gentleman carpenter', the slightly nutty old guy who lives in a stately home and makes things. That culture was the prevailing culture at school in the 1950s though. Everyone studied carpentry. My best friend really understood cabinet-making, without being a beard-stroker. You know, I continue to associate that friendship with a specific place. I have very direct psycho-spatial associations, and the area in which he died, too, will always be bound up with memories of him. We shared a studio down in Dalston Grove in 1969. I used to live there. I watched Heygate [the Tim Tinker-designed housing estate in Elephant & Castle, built 1974, now under demolition] and Aylesbury [the largest housing estate in Europe, in Walworth, built 1974] being built, and applauded. I believed that was the future. And it's very odd now to be old enough to see and to comprehend social failures. You realise that all architecture is made in a space that is barely thirty years long. You can't fold that awareness of how things work forward. It's part of the job of being in the world to have a go though. Architecture is built in that space, to be able to handle only the immediate future. But it's almost instantly in a state of fallibility. You're dealing with contingencies and fallibilities. You know I look at this handrail and, even though it is horribly constructed, there is something laudable, something moral about the motives underlying its construction.

Q. THE WHITE REVIEW — Moral?

A. RICHARD WENTWORTH — Well there's an attempt to put value into it. These joints aren't glued. They're actually excessively well welded together. There are however moments of apology where they change the language. There's a mixture of lightness and heaviness, and different types of fixing points, and it's like they forgot that they were constructing something coherent. And all that was apparent to my eye within a millisecond, and that's because I make things. I don't mind art being ugly, but it has to be wilful ugliness.

Q. THE WHITE REVIEW — Do you think that value is inherent to the energy and thought invested in constructing something?

A. RICHARD WENTWORTH — It's to a degree about the legibility of something. I think the circle and the square are both jokes. You never see a square. You see them in art but rarely elsewhere. It's like the word of God. The circle is not far off. When you see a circle you never see it as a circle, you see it as an ellipse, because it's in space. I made IDIOT CIRCLE [constructed out of coat-hangers] and there were two responses; people who were horrified that you could see that it was made semi-competently, and another group who loved the work's fallibility.

Q. THE WHITE REVIEW — You give your works titles, which seems then to encourage a textual interpretation of things. But you seem to be saying that the language of your work is expressly non-verbal, non-textual?

A. RICHARD WENTWORTH — I think I shouldn't give things titles. I sometimes cringe at it. But it's like naming the cat. There is something about the act of nomination — sometimes I really love it, like launching a ship. I remember the strangely over-celebrated little dictionary with all the sweet papers in it [TRACT (FROM BOOST TO WHAM), 1993]. I remember almost making that with my children. I remember explaining to them on long car journeys that the name of the particular confectionary couldn't have any sense of rhyming nomination. I wasn't interested in Aero. But the proposal in something like Boost or whatever was appropriate. It was a process that took place over a year or so, which began with me finding a book with a Kit Kat wrapper used as a bookmark. And I thought that it set up a really interesting space between the oral and the aural, and the word. But it was initially just idle speculation. I think a lot of my work starts from idleness.

Q. THE WHITE REVIEW — That relates back to this idea of allowing for contingency, for the outside world to interfere in the process of making art?

A. RICHARD WENTWORTH — Well yes but it also makes me feel guilty. I feel like I'm not a productive artist. I've known Anish Kapoor and Anthony Gormley since we were students and, while I don't want to be like them, I often think I ought to be more visibly productive. I had lunch a couple of months ago with Hussein Chalayan recently, who I don't really know, but he grabbed my arm at one point and said 'This man is a Mediterranean trapped inside an Englishman's skin!' and I thought 'I want to sleep with you!' It was so nice. I don't know what I'd said but I'd said something about the discomfort of being a northern European, this determination to rationalise everything. It's like not feeling you're breathing deeply enough. It's why English Modernism is so sad, because they want to get to *meaning*. I was told recently that my students say of me that 'things happen to him and then other things happen to him'. And they're right.

BENJAMIN EASTHAM
APRIL 2011

CONFLICTS OF INTEREST: FRANK O'HARA AND THE COLLABORATIVE TALENT

BY

THIRZA WAKEFIELD

ARTISTIC COLLABORATION, in all disciplines, is — and has ever been — the exception. In its unmitigated form — taking place between two or more individuals working to one end, and with the particulars of responsibility dissolved in consensus — collaboration has proven to be a versatile and available mode of artistic production. So why is collaboration given so wide a berth? That, historically, so large a proportion of collaborative works come over apologetic — mollifying their collaborative character — would suggest that it is in the *understanding* of collaborative art, and not the undertaking, where lies the issue. And for this reason: collaborative art overturns our perception of 'the artist', to which we hold fast, even if we *don't* know it.

It is important to clarify what I mean by collaboration. There are media that necessarily utilise a workforce, the craftsmanship of others, that are inherently 'collaborative' but to which, for the purposes of this article, we will not apply the term collaboration. A big-scale beehive of a collaborative endeavour, a film congregates large numbers of individuals, each a satellite contributor and specialist — in cinematography, animation, sound or wardrobe design. But if a film's achievement may be credited to individuals in titled, subsidiary roles, it cannot satisfactorily be called a collaboration. How far can a film's scriptwriter be said to have collaborated with its stunt man? There is no transaction of ideas, no arbitration; they are connected indirectly by an intermediary in the form or forms of director and producer. Collaboration in film, and to the same degree, theatre, is contingent upon a selection or hiring process; 'collaborators' are delegated to and in most circumstances work apart. In the critical theory of François Truffaut and other contributors to CAHIERS DU CINÉMA, the success (or failure) of a film is attributable only to its director, Truffaut's apiculturist 'auteur'. If I am inclined to disagree with Truffaut's solo-project take on the film industry, I am also unable to name his cameramen, his editors, his supporting casts. Ai Weiwei's SUNFLOWER SEEDS is a similar instance of the figure-headed or curated 'collective' artwork. The Beijing artist employed over a thousand artisans over five years to hand-paint the porcelain counterfeits. But it is understood that the men and women that mined, moulded and painted the miniatures — who feature in the documentary companion-piece — are not collaborators. Their collaboration is practical necessity, not aesthetic. Even so, as an artist interested in the anthropological provenance of the object and symbol — best illustrated by his photo triptych DROPPING A HAN-DYNASTY URN (1995) — it is the sense of a vestigial *community* that makes for much of the impact of Weiwei's latest work, which makes spectacle of human industry.

But when two persons jointly undertake the same, undifferentiated role — as in the case of Michael Powell and Emeric Pressburger and the Coen brothers, where the distinctions between writer, director and producer are blurred — there is real collaboration. There is equality in consensus and, importantly, no telling who did what. Collaboration, in this unmitigated form, is more common to the modern and contemporary art world, particularly among conceptual and installation artists of the last fifty years. Bernd and Hilla Becher began collaborating as early as 1959 with their square-on black and white photography of industrial landscapes, and the uniformed Gilbert & George in 1970 with *The Singing Sculpture*. Christo and Jeanne-Claude conceived many of their most famous, large-impact field works — *Valley Curtain* (1972), *Running Fence* (1976) and *The Pont Neuf Wrapped* (1985) — in Christo's name, only later in 1994 acknowledging their collaboration on every colour-textile work produced to date. Likewise, American artist Edward Kienholz became *Kienholz*, one half of a creative partnership with his wife, Nancy Reddin, when an exhibition catalogue confirmed that all his pop-installations since 1972 had been co-produced. All these artist-sets, excepting Gilbert & George, whose geminate self-representation is integral to their collaborative identity, are linked by marriage. Collaboration is a lifelong commitment. But still more interesting is the hesitation by some artists to declare collaboration. This, it seems to me, has to do with the public and institutional regard for collaborative art. By these characteristics — the familial, long-term and exclusively collaborative — the artists resemble the artist singular, and are consistent with the accepted configuration of the author-artist as solitary and hermetic. Their collaboration is somehow vitiated *and* made palatable to the public, because they are, as kin, of one mind.

It is possible to collaborate without forfeiting autonomous artistic identity. Pablo Picasso and Georges Braque did so when they co-founded Cubism. The two artists, sharing a common influence in Paul Cézanne, attracted to his geometrisation of forms and the compartmental surfaces of his paintings, began in 1908 to develop a style of painting in fidelity to what they considered the plural and cumulative nature of seeing. Painting separately — though allegedly side-by-side — on canvasses their own, Picasso and Braque worked closely in consolidation of a technique, drawing upon very disparate artistic backgrounds: Braque in Fauvism and Picasso's aspiring to the baldness of Primitivist, African and Iberian art. Their six-year collaboration was interrupted by the outbreak of war in 1914 and was not renewed, but their impact upon European art was by this time firmly established. Although it is said that Braque's paintings of this period may be mistaken for Picasso's and vice versa, each artist retained at all times his distinct artistic identity, neither one eclipsing the other. Thus, Cubism's collaborative origins never troubled anyone. Still, this particular collaboration of idea eludes the question of whether collaboration of the *material* kind — a collaboration of idea, brought to bear upon a single surface — can overcome the fixed public regard for autonomy in creativity.

That collaboration confounds a formal understanding of artistic identity is certain. Collaboration or co-authorship upends our perception of the role of artist — the monogrammed, dark-circled solipsist — and drives a wedge between ourselves and the gallants of literature and cinema, who we like to idolise and study as close as the biopic and the poster shop would allow. This may explain why collaboration is most seldom seen in poetry. It is the poet, after all — before the novelist, the painter and the filmmaker — whose contours as artist are most immovable. In poetry, above all other art forms, the cult of the individual is hardest wired, and so we may look to poetry for what determines to a lesser degree the success of collaboration in other art forms. Of all disciplines, it is in reading poetry that we are least able — or least disposed — to dissociate the artist from his work. Roland Barthes' 'Death of the Author' and T. S. Eliot's 'Tradition and the Individual Talent' partake of a long and extant tradition of critical debate as to the role and the textual presence-absence of the author. In spite of critical attempts to free the work of its writer, there remains an appetite for artists' letters and literary criticism of a biographical bent. This tenacity of the author resides even in the metonymic association of author and works — we read Salinger; 'I'm getting stuck into *Gaskell*' — and in Harold Bloom's canon like so much statuary. Since the advent of Confessionalism in the 1950s, and with it the relaxing of the propriety of poetic subject, the interval between poet and reader has grown narrower still. This often morbidly confessional poetry dominated the latter half of the twentieth century in reaction to Eliot's crepuscular impersonality and the New Critical school, whose objectifying, non-contextual reading of poetry rent — impermanently — the author from his text. In Robert Lowell's *LIFE STUDIES* — to which the term 'Confessional' was first applied in 1954 — and in the work of Anne Sexton, poetry is constituted *a priori*, it is partial. It had no longer to be so emphatically defined by its content nor observant of an objective tablature. This generation believed there could be poetry in the *saying* of it; it mattered less how. (So much so that rhymed and metrical verse have still to recover their footing.) The movement thus intensified not only authorial presence in poetry but the relationship between the author and his readership.

There is a sense when reading poetry that the poem is *made* in the reading, that it is incomplete until a reader elects to engage reflexively with the poetic subject. A poem is between-two, transitive; it is the systole-diastole exchange of thought and feeling. Like Venn diagram or the overlapping circles of D. H. Lawrence's ideal love — 'when it is whole, it is dual' — reader and poet are apart in concordance. This doubling, that is itself a collaboration between poet and reader, complicates the possibility for collaboration between poets. With the addition of a third party, and the outnumbering of poet to reader, collaboration becomes collusive. This is the first impediment to the reading, as to the writing, of collaborative poetry, and of the few examples that exist, collaborators have either safeguarded *against* or exploited (by inclusion of the reader against a wider audience) the conspiratorial nature of literary collaboration.

If, in visual art, collaboration masquerades as autonomous creative enterprise, in poetry it is, historically, subversive. Collaborative poetry has in almost all cases accompanied the undermining of literary covenant. The French Surrealist movement of the 1920s encouraged collaboration among its members in defiance of a prohibitively conservative literary establishment. Surrealist publications — *LITTÉRATURE* and *LA REVOLUTION SURREALISTE* — collated new writing techniques. Among them was André Breton's *cadavre exquis*, a work of prose or poetry composed by the contributions of several authors in turn. But if collaboration is iconoclastic — not existing for its own sake but borne along by intellectual radicalism — it must also be transient. This historical precedent, the identification of collaborative art with provocation, has prevented its proper assimilation by the literary establishment and the reading public.

The poets of the New York School — John Ashbery, James Schuyler, Kenneth Koch and Frank O'Hara — are a rare, perhaps even unique, example of a literary collective to have collaborated extensively and without political agenda. Ironically named by John Bernard Myers, an art dealer and owner of Manhattan's Tibor de Nagy gallery, the New York School was less programmatically innovative than the Surrealists, and not so earnest or self-regarding as its French namesake the École de Paris. The group were foremost friends, each possessing a distinctive style — Ashbery's involute, thickly-textured poetry cannot easily be confused for the jerky kinetics of Kenneth Koch — but all four shared an enthusiasm for collaborative enterprise that stretched beyond their small circumference. The New York School approached collaborative compositions with the same seriousness as they applied to their own solo efforts. Collaboration was considered to be a natural development of personal undertaking, and appealed to the playful creativity and explorative intellects that first drew them together. Perhaps inspired by Breton's *SURREALIST MANIFESTO*, which urged the writing of 'false novels', it took Ashbery and Schuyler fifteen years to compose — piecemeal and together in-person — their comic novel-length character-study *A NEST OF NINNIES*. But it is interdisciplinary collaboration for which the New York School are most renowned. These collaborations were so many they were commonplace: pre-empting the so-called 'happenings' of the following decade, the New York School took to a collaboration with the same abandon as a weekend in the Hamptons. Their collaborators were as varied as their social element, encompassing both first and second generation Abstract Expressionist painters, composers and filmmakers, and dancers of the New York City Ballet. Their collaborative enterprising brought them into frequent contact with the alumni of North Carolina's Black Mountain College, a progressive educational institution, established in 1933. Although short-lived, closing its doors in 1957, the college taught the value of interdisciplinary collaboration, drawing the likes of John Cage, Merce Cunningham, Willem and Elaine de Kooning to its faculty and launching students Robert Rauschenberg and Cy Twombly upon the Manhattan art scene.

But of the four, the New York poet most drawn to interdisciplinary collaboration was Frank O'Hara, a galvanising presence in the art world, whose readiness to collaborate was expressive of a fêted generosity and serious-mindedness about the work of others. Composer Morton Feldman described the poet as seeming to 'dance from canvas to canvas ... from poem to poem — a Fred Astaire with the whole art community as his Ginger Rogers.' O'Hara made STONES, a series of charcoal prints with Larry Rivers, recently exhibited in a Tibor de Nagy retrospective; provided text for Alfred Leslie's eccentrically subtitled film, THE LAST CLEAN SHIRT; and wrote the lyrics for Ned Rorem's THE QUARREL SONATA. He worked most regularly with the poet Bill Berkson on what he called 'actual collaborations line for line', publishing a collection of poems (HYMNS OF ST BRIDGET) and devising over the Atlantic FLIGHT 115: A PLAY, OR PAS DE FUMÉE SUR LA PISTE on O'Hara's portable typewriter. Their work together is, like O'Hara's poetry, peripatetic and permissive of the emergent thought. O'Hara's poetry recognises intention as illusory and is attentive, instead, to ulterior possibility — to any new idea or image — that may arise from the setting-down of thought, and from the ill fit of word to feeling. This and his precipitate approach to composition made him more adaptable to the collaborative mode, which asks that a collaborator concede to some degree those principles that would ordinarily govern his or her work. No poet could be better suited to this than O'Hara, who confided to Koch in 1956, 'Acting isn't so bad, actually, it makes you feel inadequate just like poetry.' Inadequacy was to Frank O'Hara as deprivation was to Philip Larkin: incitement to write. But O'Hara's interest in other disciplines was accessory and implement to his poetry. Writing to poet Gregory Corso of the collaborations between writers and jazz musicians of the 1950s, he confided: 'I don't really get their jazz stimulus but it is probably what I get from painting... that is, one can't be inside all the time, it gets too boring and you can't afford to be bored with poetry so you take a secondary enthusiasm as the symbol of the first.' For O'Hara, collaboration was a catalyst, a stimulant, a means of faster negotiating and refining those impressions and images that would in due course populate his poems. This is not to diminish the value of collaboration — because it is tributary — but rather to demonstrate its importance. Collaborative practice, close-conference with another, quickens the creative mind and facilitates invention. For O'Hara, at least, the creative initiatives of others, even those at variance with his own, kept off a debilitating lethargy that endangered the quality of his work.

But we would do well not to get carried away with depicting this era as one of peculiar fecundity for interdisciplinary collaboration. Al Leslie, who collaborated frequently with O'Hara, felt acutely that his critics had difficulty conceiving of an artist who worked in more than one discipline at one time; who took a second enthusiasm equal to the first: 'There's always a suspicion of anybody who works well in many disciplines. I was acknowledged in them individually, but nobody saw a way to bring them all together.' He sensed, instead, that there had to be an 'expertise' — in painting, for example — which could then justify 'forays' into alternative media. He thus considered himself an abnormality of his era: 'It was a quintessential moment in the sense that it was a kind of public exposure that I had several public voices. At that time artists were supposed to only focus on one particular area.' Leslie's insight is surprising because this period of the 1950s is commonly registered to be one of artistic association, and the free-traversing of disciplines. Described by Bill Berkson as 'a one-man movement', Frank O'Hara certainly made it seem so. But perhaps it wasn't that way. While there may have been cross-pollination of ideas, loose and sometime collaborations, the interdisciplinary artist was at this time an exception.

Nevertheless, the literary collaborations of the New York School — the burlesque *A Nest of Ninnies* and the three-legged poetry of Berkson and O'Hara — succeed by creating a cohesive poetic-narrative voice, and because we cannot help but share in their exuberance for the co-authoring process. Both works are attractive because we are drawn into closer engagement with the nature of their production; they are auto-deconstructive, art and commentary both. What is more, they antagonise the belief that poetry is rarefied; that there is the genesis of idea in solipsism. But it may also be the case that they succeed because they are *comic* works, and comic works do tend to discourage critical opinion and so escape the eyeglass. What has yet to be discovered is whether poetry may be affective *and* co-authored.

Might it not be a simple case of readerly adjustment? We do not, on first reading, read falteringly through T. S. Eliot's 'The Waste Land' second-guessing the interstices of Ezra Pound's edit, and our first reaction to Raymond Carver's *What We Talk About When We Talk About Love* isn't to wonder what might have been excised by his editor, Gordon Lish. Or is it rather the responsibility of a new generation of poets to reform our understanding of the origins of poetry? To re-examine the inherited formulations of poet-theorists such as William Wordsworth — for whom poetry is 'emotion recollected in tranquillity' — and W. B. Yeats, who is credited with the following assessment: 'Of our conflicts with others we make rhetoric; of our conflicts with ourselves we make poetry.' Why should poetry and art not derive from our conflict with others? Are the arts so fetishistic, individualist, are we so infatuated with the genius solitaire that collaboration is implausible? We would like to think not. For now, collaborative practice remains — at best, a relic of friendship — a curio, a gimmick, but not art.

CAFÉDÄMMERUNG

AND

NOTES TOWARD THE CRANE POEM

BY

JOSHUA COHEN

CAFÉDÄMMERUNG (OR ALLEN IN PRAGUE, KING OF MAY, 1965)

> It was even worse in Prague [than in Cuba]. The only reason they got upset with me — I was in Prague for a month, went to Moscow for a month, trained then to Poland for a month, and went to Prague to leave for New York. I got back to Prague on April 26 — the same day I was put on the FBI Dangerous Security List — was elected King of May on May 1, was followed around Prague until May 7, arrested, kept incommunicado, and put on the next plane to London because the minister of culture and the minister of information disapproved of an American gay beatnik, pot-smoking, mantra-chanting Buddhist (or something) being a model for Czechoslovakian youths.
>
> — Allen Ginsberg, interview

He'd been in Cuba sunning, fucking. But he'd only hugged and kissed Fidel. Reek of cigars! rum!

In that embrace, two of the great beards of our time had grown into each other: Allen's and Fidel's, they became inseparable. Grew intertwined, then knotted. Uncomfortable for all involved. Finally Castro had to call his chief executioner, the executioner came with his chief machete but instead of cutting off Allen Ginsberg's head a hipsterheaded angel of Yahweh arrived in sunglasses and porkpie hat to redirect the blade to only sunder their beards.

Fidel put Allen on the first flight to Czechoslovakia. Allen brushed his smokestained suit before disembarking. He still had Fidel's hairs on his lapels, that's what he declared to Customs.

Students of the Polytechnic School, even a few faculty members, remember: the first sign they had of Allen's coming was the beard. It was edged out the window of the plane. Out the window of the taxi from Ruzyně (airport), as if a flag for a new order, his novy kingdom. But he was not yet King. It was still April.

Allen's beard was not a religious beard, yet neither was it a beard of dereliction, of dissolution, a lazy facial hirsuteness — the mark of a man who did not care about appearance. It fell under none of those categories, contra surveillance and Nomenklatura speculation. Truth is, Allen's beard had always been there, and his face grew from it — Allen's face, his head, *that* was the effort, that was the true growth, it was conscious, its expression beatifically made.

The beard was of a million fingers of vermilion, ten thousand threads of rust and purple prose sunrays, flecks of recitative spittle and a dusting of light sporelife, the yellowed ermine fuzz that forms around immemorial potatoes.

That expression: comic, fishily bulging lips and eyes, exophthalmic but glassesed, Jewish. He'd gotten chubby during his Havana sojourn. All those fried plantains and anus. Also Allen was balding above. And he was ancient, he was forty.

What comes between men is the beard. The beard is philosophy, hairs on the face are a politics, what keeps one brother from another. What hides, what obfuscates. The beard is that thick fat wilderness where miscommunication causes lives to come to their ends — the forbidding forest in which compatriots would be shot, had been shot, for example outside Moscow toward the east.

But this was Prague, Western enough to expect Allen's Yiddish to be understood as inept German. Here he would be crowned King of May — 'which is Kral Majales in the Czechoslovakian tongue,' he wrote in a poem about that experience because he wrote poems about all his experiences (it wasn't an experience until it was a poem). The poem was called *Kral Majales*, and it was called that because Allen could not be bothered with diacritical marks — it should be KRÁL MAJÁLES, with vowels long like pleasure — here are its essential lines:

> For I was arrested thrice in Prague, once for singing drunk
>   on Narodni street
> once knocked down on the midnight pavement by a
>   moustached agent who screamed out BOUZERANT,
> once for losing my notebooks of unusual sex politics dream
>   opinions,
> and I was sent from Havana by plane by detectives in green
>   uniform,
> and I was sent from Prague by plane by detectives in
>   Czechoslovakian business suits,
> Cardplayers out of Cézanne, the two strange dolls that
>   entered Joseph K's room at morn
> also entered mine, and ate at my table, and examined my
>   scribbles,
> and followed me night and morn from the houses of lovers
>   to the cafés of Centrum —
>
> And I am the King of May, which is the power of sexual
>   youth,
> and I am the King of May, which is industry in eloquence
>   and action in amour
> and I am the King of May, which is long hair of Adam and
>   the Beard of my own body

On each table they place a saucer, on each saucer they place a cup (demitasse), next to each they put a shotglass of tepid water, a pitcher of cool cream. A napkin. On the napkin, a spoon. In the spoon, reflection of.

Nothing more sexual than a spoon except, perhaps, fire.

An ashtray like an ancient castle defence, like a ceramic turret with a cigarette, newly rolled and licked sealed, wedged into a crenature. A box of matches adjacent. (Waiterwriters should have been rolling cigarettes since morning.)

This is turning into a poem, a list poem, a list.

Alcohol will be made available only after the festivities.

Waiterwriters are informally required to be familiar with an array of aesthetic trivia: Alcestis was a Grecian princess and a tragic play in Greek, Bucephalus was a horse while boustrophedon is the alteration of written lines in two different alphabets, one line – in this alphabet, the Roman – reading left to right, another line reading right to left in another alphabet, such as that of the Arabs or Jews. Rodin, a sculptor, employed Rilke, a poet. The decadent jazz 'standard' SEPTEMBER SONG is most often performed in the key of C Major, which is without black notes and so is, like the majority of Slavonic jazz interpretations, all white. Blake. Portraiture the lowest form of flattery, viz. Picasso's formalistically distorted Mme. Stein. Marijuana grows wildly in America, Mexico, Cuba, from where Allen's flown on the wings of a beard that has nine wings like the leaves of a cannabis leaf. 'O it's a long long while from May to December / but the days grow short when you reach September.' Rilke was born in Prague but denied it. Near the Main Post Office. Jindřišská ul. AKA Heinrichsgasse. From which he mailed himself to Paris c/o Rodin, a sculptor.

Kafka rarely escaped.

Incidentally, what was the inspiration for Kafka's giant bug? A local roach or desiccated scarab, displayed in a case at the Natural History Museum?

No, your server will tell you.

It was a coffee bean, imported from South America, future continent of émigrés and Mengele.

A bean no more impressive than a prostitute's gnawed thumbnail, bifurcated down the middle, segmented as if an insect. Dead. It is ground in a grinder, chewed by blades into a powder — a fine powder like ashes.

Then warm water is pressured through the powder set in a straining mechanism: some form of filtration, whether a paper pyramid or plastic colander cone. Thiswise the powder flavours the water — and so the water becomes coffee to drink.

To keep you up at night, writing. The only time you have to write, all night.

The cigarettes are rolled of cheap Cuban tobacco. Rilke rarely smoked, Kafka never did.

Annotations for a translator: One drinks a coffee. One reads a poem. One writes one.

However, kaddish must be *howled*.

At noon tomorrow, the waiters who write who are also the writers who wait will pause their preparations at the sound of a huge Slavic Om: the hum of the horny crowd from the Polytechnic massing in the squares — (polytechnic means the students can be taught anything: they can be taught engineering, mathematics, from which they might learn napping, dissent) — awaiting a word from their King.

They claw the cobbles, awaiting a word from Král Allen.

Krallen (meaning, in German, 'claws').

Kafka on Prague: 'this old crone has claws' (*Dieses Mütterchen hat Krallen*).

'Bouzerant' is misspelled Czech, should be buzerant: derogatory term for 'homosexual' (in the sense of '*buggerer*').

Awaiting word from Allen:

A howl, or kaddish in its memory —

Do not think this was his first kinging. Thirty years before, Allen's crazy mother brought him across the river parted with a bridge, they took the rotten yellow bus into the city of York and there walked south through its gross & inimitable streets:

(*list poem number two*)

and there on the streets were Whitman addicts

and there were Latin men picking noses with knives

    (and which was a switch and which a butterfly

knife?)

and there on the street was a fish scaled like brass knuckles flopped its guts open on the sidewalk alongside crumbs of pumpernickel bread that are to the pigeons, loaves

and there were Negroes as tightly wound and unreliable as the G-string on a dreadnought guitar

(experimental) wirehanger-mobilemaking milkmen whose righteous *char-ity* resembled that of Engels to Marx unfigureouttable furniture movers (repomen) of the Baltics or Balkans and through mixed marriages both Polack florists glassyeyed rheumatic glaziers a chimp with erotically long toes who'd done silent movies but was now retired living alone with a chandling harem of Swedish sisters and their midget Armenian pimp, and this was just Union Square — not named as many think for labour unions like radical politics like why Allen and his mother were here but because this was where two major streets once came together, entered into Union: Broadway & the Bowery.

Allen and Mother passed the above on their way to an unlit storefront. They entered, stepping over the threshold — Ma lugging Allen over the threshold — that was only a drunk slumped who was also the meeting's watchman and the, if also unremunerated until now, lookerupper of skirts. Allen's mother's vagina was violently dark and its lips clapped like erasers to flatulate chalky dust as she walked. She'd been a teacher in Jersey public schools before she crazied enough to stop wearing panties — but in this meeting, because meeting it is, Allen will be teaching. He's passed up to the front, a low stage. Hands hands all hands. He stands on a chair atop the stage facing his audience, he's already the pro, his passion has been from the very Genesis beginning memorised, stagy. He has no text with him, nothing to read from on cards or to crib in ink from the palm, he makes his memory as he goes along, he improvises. Come what may to mind or tongue. Care not lest ye be cared about, in the wrong way. *L'chaim* and damn the thoughtcops (later his epithets would grow stronger)!

He talks about socialism.

He talks about (another poem) everyone being equal but

he talks about (no *but*) the Worker the workers of the

Spanish Civil War the purges

the poyges! (what a family they were)

the show trials the executions of Zinoviev and Kamenev

and ev ev ev

Amen because Stalin has begun to sour around here,

despite

how he mentions the Eighth Congress Molotov the Nazis and Hitler and how Stalin though appreciated world Jewry at least Molotov did because Marx was Jewish and,

Allen recites: 'the Jewish people gave many heroes to the revolutionary struggle & continue to produce more fine & gifted organisers than any other,' etc.

Nachas, nachas.

Namaste.

Irwin! Irwin!

(Ginsberg's given name, whose meaning is 'boarfriend' — *Ir* 'boar', *win* 'friend' — so you can understand why he went with Allen because what Jew befriends a boar?)

And the audience loved it! They weren't a movement so much as an audience who loved and applauded Irwin Allen and hugged and kissed Irwin Allen and everybody everybodied him and this audience love told Irwin Allen that he needed to be loved and this need to be loved made Irwin Allen a poet though it was only the fact — the fact! that he hated that he needed to be loved that made him a good poet, as if against his will, as if against his nature (Europeans like the socialists applauding him had *will*, American hippies such as he would become had *nature*), but that night he was still an acersecomic toy boy reciting by rote the words of grownups.

Ma was triumphant — walking him out of the meeting through Union Square toward the buses where rumbling home they'd plan amid the empty seats to plan his next address.

Vendors swarmed the square but there was nothing to vend. A Muscovite roasting his own hairy nuts. A clutch of wilted daffodils, bouquets of week old leek, parsley, parsnip, turnip, onion, garlic. Potato. Soup starters, starches. A Chinaman making shapes out of newspapers, he was folding the morning editions into odd origami if not to sell then just to pass the time not selling: foldbeaked birds perched to graze upon the backs of wild animals that grazed on ink, a crown.

Two cents of a nickel, celebration!

Ma bought Allen that crown made out of frontpage, a headline for banded jewels: FRANCO REFUSES IMMUNITY TO FOREIGN REFUGEE SHIPS. She paid the man like all other men then kinged her son, who ruled her world already. Allen kept his head down, had to hold his new crown down on his head as he walked toward the bus stop, the other hand in his mother's hand then in his mother's pocket – 'foreign refugee ships,' two sails stooped by the wind.

Allen was not allowed to leave Prague with the crown the students gave him. The police, the secret police if that is not a paradox to speak of them, confiscated the cardboard party favour before deporting him, just like Castro kicked him out of Cuba (just as Generalísimo Franco banished poetries in Basque, Catalan, Galician/Portuguese). For masturbating publicly, for stroking off on hotel balconies with a broomstick up his ass, biting a tape recorder to mute his pleasure: Allen, for that no glitter garland, for such no diadem.

The crown ended up on a hat rack at the headquarters of the Czech Secret Police.

If that is not a paradox to speak Czech of them.

Street, Konviktská.

Allen was in Prague for only a month.

The following people were in Prague longer than Mr. Ginsberg: Rilke, Kafka, Pan Novotný who drove a taxicab and was born in the town and died in town and was a plumber too (unofficially, for friends and his wife's extended family), and never deserved the poem that was written for him because he was unambitious, which is to say he was honest.

Sources are not saying he slept with Allen but.

He didn't leave the room till morn.

(And was the author of a novel on the subject 'a marionette from Josefov,' that came alive at midnight to restore the interiors of neglected provincial churches – unpublished, unless you count three copies mimeographed by friendly brewery assistant Jiří.)

A last word about your wraiters.

F

During breaks or at night, they wrote their poems and stories with pen on the papers they used to roll cigarettes. They rolled cigarettes for Allen with these papers and he smoked them, unknowingly, perhaps, or perhaps this too, like fluid exchange during sexual intercourse, was a form of smuggling, an alchemical samizdat — a way of internalising their precious words for later disbursal as coughs, sneezes.

Cancer, cancer, one for each lung.

Allen took their words into his lungs. He filled his wine barrel chest with verse.

His last Prague afternoon the King already crowned — about to be dethroned through deportation, about to abdicate to London — sat in the Ambassador's lobby café, uncomfortably. Agents surrounded. Critics (agents) hid behind walls, their aperçus were wallpaper patterns. In the kitchen, Allen's wraiters spit more of their poems into his coffee, thick and heavy poemspit in his coffee they served him cold because they loved him — he was their King, and they wanted to make his own poetry even better by making the life that wrote it worse.

F

NOTES TOWARD THE CRANE POEM

> I never met Hart Crane. I read of his death in 1932, when he jumped off the stern of a ship called the Orizaba. It was 24 hours north of Havana, and in my will there is a codicil that I should be buried at sea as close as possible to the point where he jumped overboard, because I had a great reverence for Hart Crane as an artist.
> — Tennessee Williams, interview

I.
Time to write that poem about Hart Crane (dates). Specifically a poem about his death by suicide. On that ship off the Florida Coast, *off* that ship *on* the Florida Coast. A poem I've been wanting to write for decades since I turned 32....

I want to record/*prisión* in poetry the moment from when Crane last touched ship's railing to when he the poet hit water to drown. This last moment freefalling of life being the freefall of *meaning*, words being dropped in space, through space, words dropping away from one another into watersilence — breaching sense once last — then again sinking below: into incoherence.

the incoherent water

Hope —
    To write my Hart Crane Poem in stages three:
    One, Crane leaps despondent from rail of boat.
    Two, Crane hits the water and fails to float.
    Three, my failed homosexuality.

I first read Crane in college, nothing interesting there, on the verge of dropping out of college, nothing interesting there either. Crane was my Whitman and Whitman was Crane's Whitman. That he wasn't fashionable then, he wasn't trendy (1967), I didn't care a whit, man — my hair was long and thin and my girlfriend — Lucky Sue — was longer and thinner. Crane died at the age at which I began to take myself seriously as a poet. Now I'm almost 64 and have been heterosexual my entire life, a reluctant heterosexual born 1946.

Im a mediocre man / but not from the Middle West

'Show don't tell' teachers tell their writing students at NYU (where I've taught), but: I've been trying to write that poem about H.C.'s suicide for as long as I've been trying to be gay, voraciously trying and now as my stars and stripe flag — I who've never married but only last week took my first pill for a hard-on — now I find I can't because I haven't yet addressed —

F

apostrophised —

told about 'the role of homosexuals in my life'

as the phrase goes, Some Of My Best Friends Are Gay but more than that almost all my friends best or not have been gay and certainly I'm the only (well-known, well-published) good poet of my generation never able to — no I can't write prose about It either. Copy such as would be cosy in the New York TIMES.

Which did not publish an obituary for C.

Orizaba
Abaziro
Orizabaziro —

The name of the boat — the ship — he'd taken before: the same ship that had brought our poet to Cuba those years ago, how many? to that island off Cuba — Isle of Pines — where he staged his first suicide attempt when he was 15 (this the first trip on which cornkid C. ever saw the sea: he was born in Ohio but his father the wealthy candymaker owned a vacation house on the Isle).

Orizaba is also the name of a mountain, a volcano (dormant), third highest in North America.

And don't say *ship*, say *oceanliner*? Which like a poem lines the ocean?

Meet me in Havana
Café *LA DIANA*

He'd been living in Mixcoac, suburb of Mexico City, with Peggy Cowley (Malcolm's ex-wife).

He used her to turn himself hetero and enact with her his parents' marriage. She used him for everything not that. She described the sea C. jumped into as 'a mirror that could be walked on'. Surprise — that line is not original with her.

Onboard the liner C. was unregenerate (which is degeneracy without hope).

He tried to fuck a crewmember, who blackened his eye into an orifice. And so the drunk's depressive leap.

If he couldn't be 'a man' — macho — he shouldn't be at all.

S.S.ORIZABA was returning to New York from Mexico, stopping in Cuba. April 1932.

C. had just lost his straight virginity to Cowley, Xmas Eve 1931. '*The Jazz Age Officially Ended!*'

Meet me in Havana
At Café Diana

Took skyblu pill / and dribbled thrill

Katherine Anne Porterhouse. *Jazz Age had no politics but gin / Homosexuality a sin* Depression turning Guggenheims into Aztecs and Mayans (no one had any cash for poetry, no one had clock enough for poems). Too much damn Marxist archaeology!

(Gloss: both C. and Katherine Anne had initially come to Mexico on Guggenheim Fellowships.)

Cold sissywinds blowing
the minds of Meheeco
                              rattle bones, tattle home, c/o Chagrin Falls

Dear John,

My one time South of the Border I did it all wrong, staying in hotels too clean and expensive and reading in expat bars translations of Octavio Paz. It was a December escape from NYC after finally a real book advance came through (that nonfiction dunger I shouldn't have dunned about the history/mythos of Coney Island), $300 airfare roundtrip from JFK to Mexico City but later I flew from there in a smaller plane to Cancún to meet my aunt at the mythical all-inclusive resort

Gertrude Berg (famous last sighting):
'[C.] walked to the
railing, took off his
coat, folded it neatly over the
railing
            (not dropping it on
deck), placed both hands on the
railing,
            raised himself on his
toes, and then dropped back again'.

two minutes to noon/two minutes after
he dove into the Tropic of Cancer

                              (dove — *swanned/plunged*)

F

no buggery or bjs
could get him out of pjs

                              (he wore the coat
                                   over pjs —
                         nympho lympho alcohol*hic*)

The resort watered its tequila, scrambled its eggs from powder and only had white toast, promiscued its women after dinner at nightly dances (Divorcées' Choice). The visit to Cancún was utter chance, I was there in Mexico City and, lonely and wanting to surprise her with incongruity as freedom, called Mom who duly alerted said you absolutely have to be in touch with Aunt Sara — who just happened that week to be wintering in widowhood, permanent winterhood — touching off a spat of expensive phonecalls across two countries resulting in me not wanting to go but going (Mom: 'It can't be that far if it's the same country, you both could use the company, it would just be polite'.). I'd read all the books I brought, all my clothes were filthy, I didn't take off my bathingsuit from Sunday to Sunday — and so you can imagine the fucking chafe the fucking rash around my crotch and inner thighs (forget this as a section but still, about the resort — *the excess impressed*

Folding coat over rail
before suicide prevails
explanation: fastidiousness or drama?

To stand on highest rung
below the yellow bung
and think: *If only I
could drink it! could drink it!*

Last buss of shoe of rail
as overboard he Cranes —
         Hart, heart — gorgeous Jorge & sailor Danes —

         *to love sailors on leave
         is to love men who leave*

Star sun above,
char sun below.
What reflection ever lasted?

F

And what current has ever slowed?
And which shark has ever fasted?

The eschat tap of toe to steel,
the slippered slip to shipless keel —
the hull of sky, Old Mizzentop,
erect yourself against the day!
Prove gravity to depthlessness
by appled drop, by falling gay
and thus in flux, flummox heaven
by being not one or both again.

      As Hart Crane falls only faller
      shall he be not baller or 'straight'
      or even late to Paradise!

      As Crane tumbles New York crumbles.
      ... *skyscape crumpled to tickertape* ...
      No parade shall he have but wind.

A bridge bodied, a span unspun,
single cable to grasp at sun,
though the supports have rotted out
    and suspension is suspended
    until metaphors assert the law
    and come to spout that daylight's ended.
    And with it search and so lush stars,
    are by foghorn called to further bars.

    burnt and from then on I had to wear a dopey gift shop sombrero, moisturise my thighs so regularly I couldn't go swimming (swimming also burned — when I had to salve myself I sent Aunt Sara off to the buffets early telling her to get good seats). At this resort whose name and latitude escape me — they wouldn't matter but neither should my forgetting imply any intimation of superior gringoness, just the recent leaks and blowholes in the brain — I didn't share a bed with Aunt Sara but *we did share the room*, twice the size of my then-apartment (I was still Downtown, Seventh Street and living in a sublet just down from McSorley's with Vietnamese grad student Lily I met at the library, she had a boy's haircut and wore ballet flats even in January, she liked sex from behind but only vaginal and squeezing her own juices and sandwiches, she ate only sandwiches pb & j and grilled cheese with wild honey and her poetry — despite that once she said over rye/swiss tuna melts and wheatgrass but without any sense of how imbecilic this would've sounded even if her mouth hadn't been fully fishy, 'Frank O'Hara means like goddamned everything to me' — was timid, precious, short very short and, like goddamned, in no way confessional about her own experience but rather confessional about other people she either knew but never introduced me to, I doubt it, or about other people she wholesale invented, characters with their own personisms wholly unbelievable:

One poem was about an overdose, another about an overdose, a third with 'a jeep pileup on Fire Island', yet another on the theme of Autism

II.

... (and these were my only three experiences) ...

J. I'd head for his house after school and we'd sit in his den and look through his father's porn mags — straight porn mags, porn mags with women, PLAYBOY was still a year or two in the future and anyway too tame, we're talking MODEL PARADE, BRIEF, EYE, a whole buncha cartoon affairs, what were called 'Tijuana Bibles' — sitting on separate facing couches and masturbating together, never each other. Until his father came home from plumbing or mother from playing bridge. The couches were yellow and because easily stained covered by plastic that made creaks and chary groans like doors opening along with our motions — we thought someone was always peeking in, about to enter. J. always used as lubrication some brand of moisturiser, or I guess we didn't call it moisturiser back then, better Vaseline (I should say petroleum jelly), while I never used anything, I never used anything at home either. Even to this day, which habit's regular, it's just bare dry hand. Sometimes bare dry *hands*. But still bare, still dry. Him jacking, me jacking too, but at half attention (full hardness) — I couldn't focus on anything but that lube he pulled from its tub balanced on couch's arm, that lube whose whiteness or off whiteness Melville should've lived to describe (sperm! sperm! avast 'a midnight sea of milky whiteness') — Whiteness that made the lube look like cum already. In both our other hands were clumps of tissue ready. Masturbation felt good but lubrication felt like you were treating yourself too well. I did not love myself enough for lube, I didn't self-love enough and so abstained.

A. (who is just J. in another guise: taller and tanner, in better worked out shape, two years after taking up track and field, junior varsity tennis and weights, fifty situps a night every night, thirty odd pushups) jerked me off on a bus ride back from a youth group summer camp, the youth group was Socialist/Jewish, Labour Zionist in funding. This handjob coming after two weeks of woodsy flirtation, common showers ass-grabbery, flipping bunks at flashlit midnight after the exhaustions of communal masturbation. Your typical circle jerks, your typical one over grab your partners, Ooky-cookie chocolate chippy, He Who Laughs Last, drunken (alternately blind) pirate, etc. Anything to distract from all that faux orienteering (can you find north from south? or start a fire with a single match?), singalongs with mallow roasts, arts & farts in which I carved half a duck decoy then grew bored. An August night and the bus splashed through the darkness. We sat in the back – the waaay back, the rumbleseats – as the trees made vertical lanes against the windows and he made vertical with me. Up and down the rumble, I didn't touch him, I pretended to be asleep. Perhaps also he cupped my hairless balls or I cupped them for him, for me. I came in three large splurts onto the seatback in front of me somewhere around Welcome to Saratoga Springs – I opened my eyes for the cum and saw the sign, 'The Spa City' – the cum dripped and, we were still hours away from the synagogue's parking lot where my father would meet us in the Plymouth, dried. *Writing it now that word is unfathomably dirty*, ply mouth ply your mouth ply my mouth, *never thought of it that way* .... We spent the rest of the trip naming the state the stain's shape reminded us of: it trickled from some sorta splotchy Midwesterner, Ohio, Illinois, 'The Land of Lincoln', to a sizeable California, Bay Area giving way to LA, and then hardened longer, like Mexico Herself. And here is Mexico City and there is Vera Cruz. (OK, also A.J. put his mouth on it once.)

Finally, and this was much more recently, I read in Berlin three years ago (never describe a poetry reading), and afterward my German translator Ch. – a Frau, no, no, a frowsy girl – asked if I wanted to have a drink and I said, Yes, that being the polite response and so drinks were had in the hotel lobby. As we toasted with round number two her bag gave a burp, she'd received a text message, which the Europeans call SMS (standing for 'short message service'), she blushed as she read it then dropped the phone back into her bag. Her endless bottomless bag, that gaping slit. I asked her, What's that? and she said nothing so I pressed the point, she finally said it was a friend who worked in film and I said, So? impress me and she said there was a party that night she'd been invited to but wasn't going to, she was with me, she said, and anyway was getting tired, but I don't think she linked the two, me and tiredness, in her mind. I said let's go and she said no, I could never bring you and I said, why not? am I not allowed? (I'm parodying my spoken German) she said, you'd hate it, no, and shook her head nervously curly like an apostrophe, suddenly I grabbed her bag, grabbed the phone and – phones working the same the world over, noting – read the message for myself, but not only was it German, it was slang abbreviated SMS German. I did understand one thing, however: Mittelweg XX, and that's what I told the taxi driver, mein Deutsch being good enough for that. Ch. always quiet became silent and obliging, in retrospect just the version of translator you want. Her rendings of my poems — make this section quick — were fine and true, I was told, but every time she read them aloud I heard darkness where I meant light, I heard heaviness, plod and stodge. It wasn't lost on me that my translator was not translating anymore, that she'd become, closer to our destination — I knew we were closer because the neighbourhood got worse, train-stationy, underlit — catatonic. The cab stopped, I paid the driver, dragged her out. There was one light on, top floor, and up we went. I hauled her up, no elevator, stairs. She'd gone limp, the door was ajar. Inside they'd been filming a porno. It wasn't lost on me either that they were, in a sense, translating themselves: the porno, judging by set and wardrobe, was the amateur porn movie adaptation of a famous regular American movie-movie. I left Ch. by the doorway, went to get drunk. Ch. sat on a sofa the entire night watching me, crying to/ignoring her friends who tried to cheer her and make her drink. Make her do some coke. A boy came to me like (insert an allusion to Classical Antiquity), offered me some and I did a line. He said, she says her career is ruined. I said, that's ridiculous. He said, how do you write poet? (Thankfully his English was *schrecklich*.) I said, how do you know Ch.? We were at university together, he said. He was an actor but allowed me to top him. We occupied the bathroom so long Ch. had to pee in the kitchen sink. Later she vomited there too.

... (*and those were my only three experiences*) ...

III.
Plastique Art:

> His body like a knife
> slashing the canvas
> of water

(like C. slashed that late portrait of himself by Siqueiros, which showed C. with downcast gaze because his eyes were mucho too powerful to paint)

Music, Music:

> His body a needle
> to the broken-
> record sea

(every biography mentions that in Mexico C. was in possession of an Orthophonic

XXII

portable, that detail culled from correspondence. To write, 'he owned a record player' would imply ignorance but Orthophonic sounds authoritative, it intimidates with brand. If the biographer's right about the phonograph, we ask, how could he be wrong about anything important?)

the stylus to the
ocean's Victrola

the brush that stabs the
sea-prepared canvas

the deep Crane's idiom to pierce
the land the bier of Ambrose Bierce

stab/pierce/slash–gash–incise–*impale* (which is more sexual?)

Bierce disappeared from Chihuahua.
Waldo Frank that Jewa Jewa:
'I warned him it was going to threaten his stability. I knew how strong the death wish was in Mexico.'
He also knew: how easier it was to get drunk at higher altitudes (Tepoztlán, *pulque*), and that socialism/communism was the answer to American strife. By the time the market's crash was felt in poetry, poets had already become political and so, it follows, marketable. Minds contracting like testicles in brine. C. was the last ecstatic, the last left Romantic, not a man of the Left but of —

Capt. Blackadder, captain of the *Orizaba*:
'If the propellers didn't grind him to
mincemeat, then the sharks got him
immediately'.

propellers being politics, *dem mincing barracooders*

Cowleys, Porter, Allen Tate
suffer the inebriate
suffer him uncelibate
Arnold, Boewe, Boff (dead of AIDS), Christkindl, Cohen, Donald, Eichenwald, Haymaker, Isakov, Jin, June, Kesztenbaum, Laurels, Manders, Mornington, Muggs, Newby, Ornaut, Palen, Quipley, Ringerling (also dead of AIDS — O to be brought

F

low by an acronym! — but his from heroin's habitual sharp-sharing), Rutman, Sonbol, Travis, Vain, Whippington-Ghernik, Yurn, Zumo: a list of homosexuals who have been friends and supporters. A list the TIMES would print — and no Sunday reviews as obituaries *pour moi*?

Ironies in steel: C. thought no great writer could be homosexual, his father, CA the sweets manufacturer of Garrettsville, later Cleveland, invented Life Savers® but then sold the patent for pennies before the money could roll in, money rolling in like waves.

    better to die before the 30s
    better to die still in your 30s
    a boat is a bridge with busted banks

Page furled loose from topside of boundless book.
    Ink shot from nib of sunrise purple pen.
        Twirling fish fleeing legendary hook.
            Midair horse farrier'd by fatboy men.

A quoin expelled from tower's break.
A coin extolled from belfry stake.
    A cigar tost a sizzling mote.
    A bottle cast without a note.

A cloudless drop of rain.
A sun set upon noon.
Brute conquest by harpoon.
    an asshole like no moon
Conquest by own harpoon.

        to break the skin with ploughing sin
            to fertilise abyssal din
      with shrieking bells and engine noise
      submerge the urge for grace and boys

I am the lowest voice of Manhattan
Drowned by the chatter of an ocean's Latin.

F

> No tide can once accommodate
> a drowning death's posterity —
> just as the ocean's never late
> and no ocean's ever early...

Heads or tails or spindrift
spume or belly flop or
boom, bombs-away adrift —
ordnance of rough trade's shore.

Bodied plummet of life's ejaculate,
puffy gray and pajamed gob,
scumming hateful hemisphere like Akron
scars the Cuyahoga — flows on.

O-hio

nomen est proem'in' est omen

The O-Hi-O

Spindrift refers to spray of waves cresting/crashing.
Findrinny means white bronze???
To leave a suicide note / is to annotate a poem.

Having sex/feelings with/for men was just not something *we could do*... ('We' meaning nice Jewboys, too nice and too Jewish and poetic for the 1960s/70s). My politics, I noxiously have a politics — poets of my generation virtually have to have a politics — have always been liberal. I believe The Gays should be allowed to marry one day (I'm writing this just after the millennium and can only hope that some transgendered transsexual future is reading me and laughing as they shake their heads and softer genital parts, but if we're all fucking one another and ourselves who'd want to read). I can't think about fucking more than once a day, once every hour it used to be — but then one day the heart will seize, the Viagra will have to stop, I take two now when I take home an intern from PARIS REVIEW and nothing then nothing — and despite how I've tried I can't seem to, *maintain* is the verb, a drinking problem. I still occasion pot, surrept a half-smoked cigarette off a student loitering outside W House or on the Mews. This semester, snooze, I'm talking Emerson the Poet. I'll come to class prepared. Tell the kids, and it's with this spiel that I'll introduce myself, 'my preparation has been Thoreau'. To quote no Transcendentalist: I'll be as outspoken as buttocks, as obscure as Thy guerdon the heaven of the Jews.

F

This has been my résumé / my CV has been my life.

ripple weird a streaming beard
skip stones to murk the sighting
broad light's broader options feared
'This closet has bad lighting.'

the ocean's water closet
snugs tight its choppy door
odd hinge binges air
buoyancy mistakes
image for metaphor
turns both tricks for passing truth

The morning I turned 60 I walked from a diner brunch on First Avenue all the way to Brooklyn across the bridge, the East River was still to the east, it was a cool fall day for falling *and do boats resemble bridges? or bridges resemble boats?* that's where I scribbled that line, stopping here and there to crib from laziness ('Cognisance whose leap commits / The agile precincts of the lark's return.'), marvelling as much at the boats and tugs below, at Liberty and the scrapers and such — when two more were still standing — as at the young and pillow-tousled strollers strolling on their strolls. C.'s bridge: 100 Columbia Heights his apartment with a view of where I walked, where he'd lived in what'd been the room of the son of the bridge's builder Roebling (though C. hadn't known this when he knew that view), huge coincidence but like all coincidence meaning nothing, as the phones say these days even without us around to talk into them, U Care? I'd never be a bard, just a renter, a lessee of language tacking tones (upstream? does that make bardic sense, or into the wind?) — I'd never be in love. Sum of my thoughts, the sum also rises (C. born the same day as Hemingway and Hemingway born in C.'s mother's hometown of Oak Park, IL) — I was on my way to see an uncle dying from his neoconservative, pro-Israel-lobby letters having been neglected by the editors of major magazines, he wanted to wish me birthday wishes. If I wanted to kill myself, I thought, I'd jump and jump from here. Like C., see me. Like the businesspeople dying their unbusiness deaths in the towers that twinned September. But even if I'd wanted to jump, I couldn't have. The Brooklyn Bridge being the-bridge-that-can't-be-jumped-off-of. There should be a foreign word for that, gephyro-unjumpoffable (*gephyra* translating bridge in Greek). You can't jump from Brooklyn Bridge at the turn of the third millennium, why? because the pedestrian walkway's located in the middle of the bridge, with the outer lanes reserved for vehicle traffic — this revealed itself to me like a solution to the Mysteries. If you jumped from the pedestrian path you'd only be run over by a car, you'd never have the privilege of the water and that's how sad life is — if it's river you want, you have to brave the car lanes, *bon courage* and bone up on aerobics, climb the netted fence and barriers, climb the lower cables graceful nimble — or else, alternately, you could drive your car off the bridge but I don't have a car and no taxi alive would take that fare....

Walk and harp the altar. Ahoy, Uncle. Walk to out me with your love — this whole island behind me a sinking ship and I'm getting off on land (another island, Long).

   Queer the plug to drain Atlantic,
   insuck the earth inverting space,
let us fall forever at the mirror
   at the queer!

Flight

Light

                  fright

right

tight

                trite

       catamite

145

I CLING TO VIRTUE

BY

NOAM TORAN
ONKAR KULAR

AND

KEITH R. JONES

INTRODUCTION / PREFACE

Memory is never in perfect control of what it preserves, and a memoirist is largely a fiction-maker. Thus, in the objects collected in this 'exhibit', an 'origin' narrative is substituted for a mass of beginnings, *in medias res*. The range of the stories told attest to the impossibility of establishing a single unifying narrative. I have therefore needed to tell several, passing all of them irrevocably through the fiction-machine of memory.

Because the real objects of memory vanish the longer we stare at them, the objects tied to the stories I tell take the form of blanks or voids, white as ghosts. For while appearing as the possessions of my family — as toys, gifts, personal effects, mementos, letters and correspondences, artefacts, even evidence — they do not, finally, belong to them alone. They are criss-crossed and penetrated by a larger world, more its possession than ours. Only at certain moments, or in specific places, can I confirm that they were, for instance, my uncle's or my grandmother's.

In 'I Cling to Virtue', the term 'family' is used to archive the constantly shifting territories and the broader historical relations, at once geographic, psychological and social, through which we might come to understand more intimately the intense upheavals and expansions of the last century. If the artefacts and artifices assembled here lead anywhere or point in any one direction, it is towards that ever disquieting haunted space between memory and memory's object.

Monarch Lövy Singh

A

I. ZENIT-E

Standing from left: my grandfather Zalman, my uncle Saul, my grandfather Bikram, my father Ranjit and me. Sitting from left: my great uncle Dudi, my mother Ava, my grandmother Judith, my grandmother Parminder. Sitting in the foreground and a bit out of focus (metaphorically as well) is my sister, Ida.

Not pictured: Uncle Max (who took the photograph).

II. 7 INCH

In the mid-1960s my father was the lead singer for Shinda, a Punjabi folk group that toured Indian musical festivals (the handful that there were) and weddings (these certainly more numerous). In the most minor places of the country, they were becoming minor stars. But in 1968, at St George's Hall in Bradford, a far-right group inspired by the National Front violently broke up a musical festival where my father's group was playing. The traditionalism of their music and the political quietism he felt surrounded by forced my father in a separate direction. He started to write and record political songs and tour more widely on his own. He met my mother backstage at an anti-war gathering she had helped to organise in the summer of 1969. He had been asked to sing his song 'Powell to the People'.

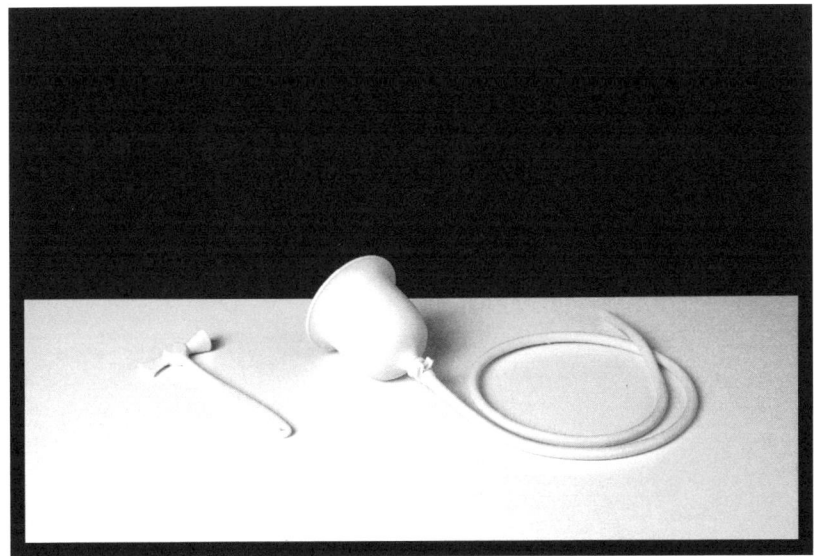

III. TOFFEE HAMMER

I only knew of my great-grandmother Lily through a story my grandmother Judith told me. My own mother adored Lily, but Judith and Lily never got on well and could hardly be in the same room without one or the other instigating strife.

Lily was a suffragette and reformist who spent much of Judith's childhood either incarcerated for various militant actions or working long hours at the Central Jewish Girls' Club. The girls in the club, whom Lily saw as her wards, came from Hoxton or, worse, Oxford Circus, and were exceedingly poor and troubled. She loved the social cause, Judith said, but hated being a mother.

Judith attempted to swim the English Channel in 1926 when she was 17-years-old.

IV. TROUT

By the time I was 13, my father had stopped sleeping in the house. Ida and I would see him every other weekend. That summer he took me and Ida up to Northumberland to go fishing on the River Wear. While he sat on the bank smoking cigarettes and watching other men's wives, Ida and I ran around in the shallows trying to catch trout with a net or, tiring of this, with our bare hands. After three days we were all bored. Then on the fourth day an absolute beauty leapt up directly in front of us. Ida and I lunged for it, wrestling with it for what seemed like an age before finally throwing it onto the shore and beating the fight out of it with a stick. We hauled it triumphantly over to our father, who, stunned somewhat and clearly absorbed by something else, became enraged, yelling at us to get rid of it. Ida and I threw the fish back into the water, where it floated, then sank. We stood there for a while, then walked to the car and waited to be driven home.

A

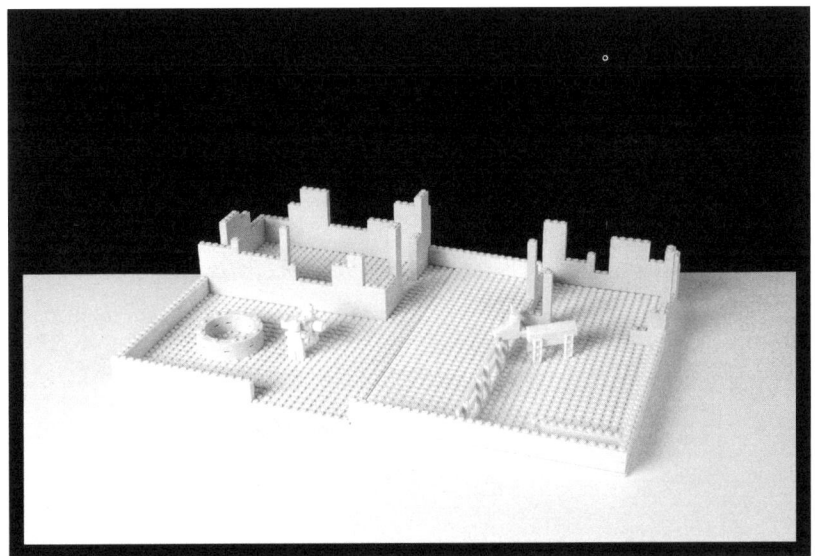

V. FARM

When I was 8 or 9, my grandfather Bikram told me a story, a secret one, that he made me swear never to retell. I could live with it only by translating it into the most expressive language I knew, which allowed me to tell it over and over again without ever speaking one word of it to anyone. It was an incident, a dramatic situation, a series of perspectives and objects and structures I built and rebuilt in varying configurations until, finally, I had come to an end of needing to figure it out. My grandfather died on a Wednesday at midday (my parents took me out of school), and I took my building bricks to the attic that evening.

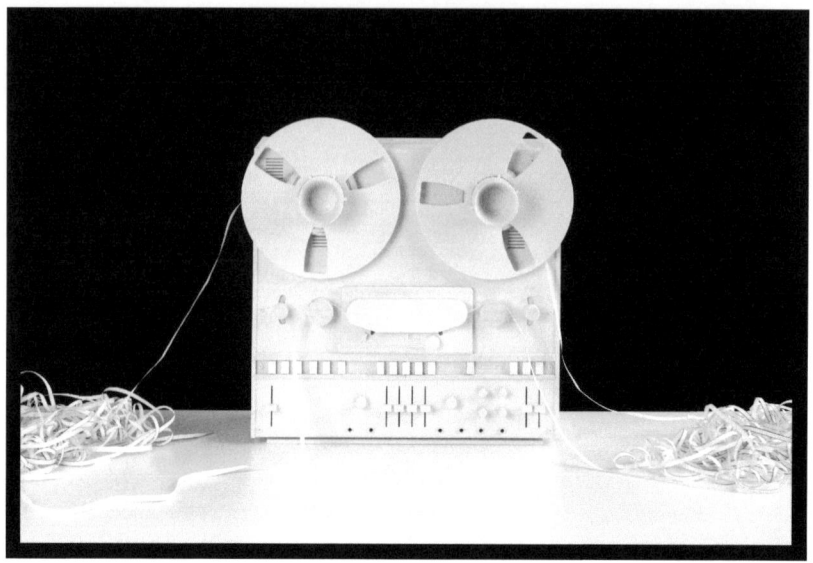

VI. REVOX A700

I remember the month of September in 1982 (I was 10-years-old) as the month that Uncle Max was tried for conspiracy and treason. His conviction rested on a series of taped conversations in which he was said to have 'conducted trade' with known traffickers engaged in provisioning 'forces and factions warring with' the British Government. This was in the aftermath of the Falklands War and my uncle's conviction (on both charges) put a sort of permanent insecurity in place for me. His trial, the sound of his disembodied voice being played and replayed in the courtroom, and the general repression and gloom of the Thatcher years all coincide for me now in a finely-threaded, eerily-animated recording device, which flipped on and off so decisively, carrying Max away from the family.

A

VII. BAR MITZVAH CAKE

In the tradition of his ancestors
MONARCH LÖVY SINGH
will be called to the Torah as a Bar Mitzvah

Please join us Saturday 26 January, 1985, 10am
Fieldgate Street Great Synagogue
41 Fieldgate Street, London E1 1JU

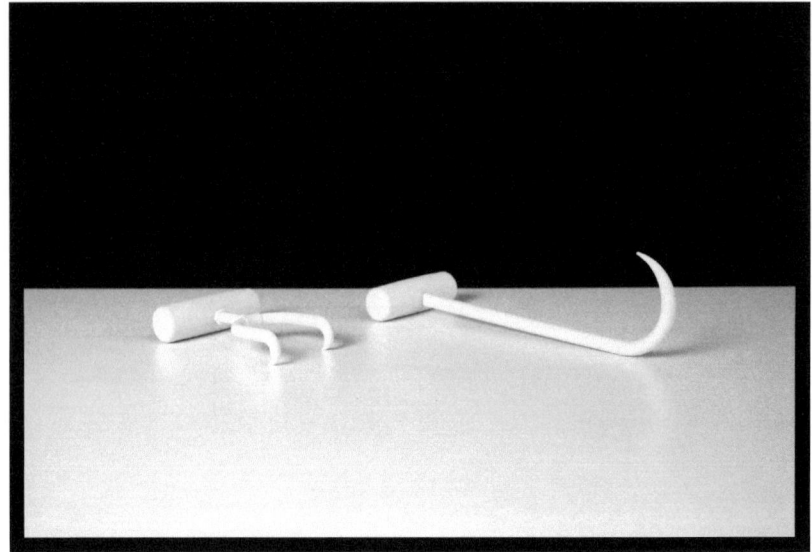

VIII. LONGSHOREMAN'S HOOKS

My grandfather came to London in 1922 as a castaway on a Lithuanian cargo freighter. He was 14-years-old. Somewhere along its passage across the North Sea he was discovered and made to clean and cook for the crew, who took a fondness to him. Once in London, he was so overwhelmed by the city that he didn't stray from the docks for four years, working when he could as a longshoreman, hoisting cargo off ships, and living hand-to-mouth in tenement houses on the Isle of Dogs. Living this way was known as 'standing on the stones' and he spoke of it as though it were the noblest thing in the world.

Then one day, seeing the woman who would become my grandmother, Zalman stepped off the docks and followed her into the city.

IX. DENTURES

Ida stole these from Maji's bedside glass of white vinegar. She dared me to put them in my mouth. Always fearless, she did it first then started talking funny. We took turns and laughed until we almost wet ourselves. Then got terribly afraid of what might happen if we got caught.

We buried them somewhere in Weavers Fields.

POETRY

BY

GRAHAM FOUST

PATRICK McGUINNESS

KIT BUCHAN

LEE ROURKE

AND

AHREN WARNER

INCREMENTAL

While waiting for sleep's good creases to my face,
I think — but also brace for dreams of lesions;
I do what I can to sink after the sun,
which would mean to go where it goes, but later,

while waiting for sleep's good creases to my face,
I think — but also brace — for dreams of lesions;
I do what I can to sink after the sun,
which would mean to go where it goes, but later.

THE BOOK OF AFTERNOON SLEEPS

That dream again: I'm hooked up to a transparent drip
full of hours, to replace the lost hours spent watching
the rain bead up the window, feeling the sex
dry on the thigh like the second skin it soon became:

the aggregate of all those public holidays we spent in bed
while your fat-fingered husband (he's light-
fingered too — how does he manage that?)
inspected troops or tractors, collected his Politburo

arse-blisters, his parade-ground pins and needles.
He'd sit in Capsia after a hard day's delegating,
blow his nose on the embroidered napkin
he'll wipe his mouth with later,

and put a two-man tail on the House Special.
While we — two boats cresting the same slow wave, or,
to put it more prosaically, two bodies carried by the same long
fuck —
'd enjoy our all-day docking at the jetty that kisses the water.

This winter, I have each gone minute of our time
stored up like city heat in bricks; in other words,
they're seeping out faster than I can hold them in.

In yet other words, they're not stored up at all.

Send more.

THE BROTHEL

I unearthed a little brothel in the spring of forty-three,
It was captained by a midwife who was ninety years of age
She produced a little bottle saying ghoulishly to me:
'you must try this new elixir, it is all the fucking rage'.

I awoke a fortnight later at a clinic underground
Where the patients all were painters, and they'd each consumed a pin
And when one was called to surgery his friends would gather round
With their brushes at the ready, to paint 'life beneath the skin'.

When the skinner-boys discovered I had swallowed no such pin
They concealed some in my dinners, and although I had no proof
I was forced to give up eating and I soon became so thin
That I fled the washy dungeon through a cat flap in the roof.

I emerged in a cathedral with a wedding in full swing,
And I sprinted down the middle (like a batsman up the crease)
And by chance I reached the altar (with the timeliness of spring)
At that moment when the vicar says '...forever hold his peace'.

I surveyed the gloomy couple with a piercing, hungry look;
It was clear he was a bastard and that she belonged with me,
So I clambered up the pulpit and I opened up the book
And declared the marriage 'filthy' using Jeremiah, 3.

All the bridal guests were cheering but the others were aghast
So I grabbed my new fiancée adding slickly 'stick with me',
And the armies of relations started fighting as we passed,
Clashing rashly into combat like the closing of a sea.

We were wedded in the crow's-nest of a galleon in Goole
Which we sailed to Vladivostok through a melted Arctic sea.
In the prow there was theatre, in the stern there was a school
And in all the world was no one who was happier than me.

– A silencing of silence, like a nunnery in mourning,
Is the sound of this adventure as its rigging turns to silk
And the linen of my vessel, in a festival of yawning,
Is dissolving in the liniment like peppermints in milk.

I am careful what I wish for, I was never very clever,
But they will not wait forever in my brothel on the land
And with sand inside my stomach I can row into the forties
Where with haughty little greetings they will shake me by the hand.

They will waive my lack of money and my ignorance of Arabic
And poetry will vanish when I moor between the caves.
And they will not make me nervous or deplete my sense of wonder;
Under muttered cups of Spanish and through stalks of oleander

I will go, and as I wander all the bats among the brickwork
And the snow beneath the trellis and the donkeys in the moonlight
And the spoons of candied ginger and the thunder and the monkeys
In the cedars and the roughness of the mattress in the night

Will be big enough to hide me from an ocean of repentance;
They will hide me from my sentence in my brothel on the hill
As I stride into my brothel they will play an old piano
(Will they have an old piano? I imagine that they will.)

They will hide me from the gallows as I paddle in the shallows
And the hollows of my spirit will be stuffed with salted cheese;
They will roast me – I will row there like a ghost upon the water
(I will need a box of matches if it's dark upon the seas.)

00.47AM IN THE MULTI-STOREY CAR PARK

Walking up to the rooftop,
Ignoring the cars, the drivers,

Inhaling the echo of concrete,
Taking it deep into the lungs,

As the city sleeps and the moon
Casts something French between

The slats: silver, like chrome, like
The forging of machinery, of cars.
[. . .]

The streets below delivering
Metallic yowls across each level.

'Whole narratives have been
Invented here: a space that

Serves modernity's whims, each
Level a secret, hidden from view.'
[. . .]

Up on the rooftop, trespassing
Space below the moon; blackness

Sticking to it like glue, each
Lifetime forgotten in the moment

(Like Pessoa's cat dreamt, you said),
When the impossible is wished true.
[. . .]

The moon sings oblivion as we sleep,
Plucking secrets from our tired eyes.

FUSELAGE THROUGH A WINDOWPANE

Caught in time, the fuselage marks the sky,
Bruising it; a line cut across a surreal canvas,
Like a scalpel through mottled skin.

A perfect frame, a vapour trail smeared across it,
No more than 45o to the left-hand reach, rising
Upwards, then disappearing into blue ash.

A repetition of scars, caught through the pane,
Flawless. Streaking upwards, as if orchestrated
By lithe brushstrokes, as thin as ribbons.

SUITE DE DANSES

for Elle

i.
Often, once or twice a day, often
more – with a slight shudder –

I conjure, involuntary, an image
of my death. More, perhaps,

a scenario: most often cancer,
as often it's my heart

giving. Sometimes something more
obscure: choking on Mozzarella.

Just now, out on the hot roof,
it was falling through and onto,

into fire. And yes, it made me think –
annoyingly, I know – of Arnaut:

Sovenha vos a temps de ma dolor...

ii.
I have an obsessional's tick
that has me tapping at my head

each time I think like this
(half to wager good luck,

half to bat such thoughts
away). Today, though, I try

to 'remember', to *Sovenha*,
Arnaut's 'suffering', which means

trying to think the pinch of fire,
pangs ripening to molten pain.

And though I can think, I think,
how he must have screamed

as those first flames nipped,
somewhere, between bubble

and peel, I come up short;
unable or unwilling to think

absolute pain, self-immolation,
the awful ecstasy of passion.

iii.
Rather, it's you – my darling – weeping
I'm thinking of. It's your lips' soft broil.

It's that I'd rather burn than fail
to comfort you with this: our long

remorseless clinch, our beatific fusion.

OPUS

That note, in Buckley's rendition
of Cohen, should exist

as the only definition for 'fucked'
– as in 'I'm fucked'.

There is a point, somewhere,
around twenty seconds in

to a Seattle-birthed song
that embodies the word 'abandon'.

So too with the dab of his foot
to the Whirlwind Selector turning

acoustic to distortion;
the sublating of silence that occurs

in that bar of the Allegro
of that Bruch Konzertstück.

There was a girl at school who'd say
I'd end up a rock star or in prison.

I'm neither, have nothing,
but an art I've been learning

too long; a subject
I've studied beyond flogged.

INTERVIEW

WITH

MICHAEL HARDT

MICHAEL HARDT IS A PHILOSOPHER AND THEORIST BEST KNOWN FOR HIS COLLABORATION WITH ANTONIO NEGRI ON A TRILOGY OF POLITICAL TREATISES — *EMPIRE*, *MULTITUDE*, and *COMMONWEALTH* — that explore the dynamics of the contemporary global order. Since its publication in 2000, the much-lauded *EMPIRE* has been touted as the 'Communist Manifesto of the twenty-first century', though Slavoj Žižek — who first made the comparison — originally left the tribute in the interrogative, as though it remained to be ratified by posterity. True to its forebear, *EMPIRE* cuts an unusual figure within the typically polemic, prescriptive genre of manifesto; its mode is one of sustained theoretical analysis animated by a forward-looking grasp of concrete political reality. Hardt and Negri have in the time since its publication secured their place among our most essential thinkers. Their work has consistently propelled dialogue about emergent political practice and has proven that there exist within the ever-fossilising Western intellectual tradition plenty of ideas and resources that are powerfully open, flexible and provocative.

  We met with Michael in his office at Duke University on a winter's afternoon. A small vase with cut daffodils in water sat on the desk, and a striking black-and-white image from the Genoa G8 Summit protests hung on the wall. During the interview he maintained, whether listening or speaking, a charming, quiet charisma. We were able to browse the spines of his library when he excused himself briefly, appealing to a quick errand to attend to elsewhere on campus. Ranged along one set of shelves set into two walls dense with hardbacks, we found copies of his books translated into more than a dozen languages: Slovenian, Portuguese, Arabic, Korean, Russian, Cantonese, Turkish and Italian, among others we couldn't readily identify. Fifteen minutes later he returned, seemingly re-energised, and we continued the interview.

———

Q. THE WHITE REVIEW — Let's start with vocation. In the 1980s you worked for some time as an engineer on energy problems and from there became involved with political activism in Latin America, but there came a moment when you decided to return to school to work on philosophy. What form did that decision take?

A. MICHAEL HARDT — [pauses and then laughs] I'm trying to edit out the simple answer, which is that I was following a girlfriend who was starting school, that being a graduate student and therefore a teaching assistant was a way of surviving when we didn't have other ways to make money. But that's only partly true. What's more true is that I was frustrated with what I perceived as the non-intellectual or even anti-intellectual character of activism in the US at the time. My activist friends in Mexico City, they were all reading Gramsci — in the groups I was involved with, that level of theoretical engagement seemed out of place. In European circles, too, there seemed to be a kind of connection with scholarly interests that I didn't find in the US, so graduate work was a way of doing the kind of theory that had an exchange with practice.

Q. THE WHITE REVIEW — You felt that the tradition of European activism could be useful to your work in the Americas?

A. MICHAEL HARDT — Well, even at the time, and this is even before any thorough familiarity with activist scenes in Europe,

I recognised and was inspired by the relationship there between theoretical and activist work, especially in the Italian activism of the 1970s and 1980s. At that time in the US, it wasn't like Deleuze or Derrida really stood in any meaningful relation to the kind of activist work that was going on. I remember reading back then that, whereas in 1968 Italian students carried around Lenin's WHAT IS TO BE DONE? to show they were radicals, in 1977 they carried Deleuze and Guattari's ANTI-OEDIPUS. As a graduate student in the US it was an opening – it was through them that I could see, for instance, how to read Deleuze politically. Of course, I've subsequently recognised that European activism struggles with similar problems about the relationship between activism and intellectual pursuits, but I think at the time it was helpful for me to imagine a kind of difference.

Q. THE WHITE REVIEW —— Naïvety can be a useful catalyst.

A. MICHAEL HARDT —— Well, it's natural to find models in contexts of intense political struggle, contexts in which intellectuals have different and sometimes more central roles. In Italy in the 1970s there was a very strong relationship between highly intellectual discourses and engagement, militancy, direct action. Seeing how it functioned there allowed me to find a way beyond what I felt as a kind of impasse in the US. Of course I've gone through different periods: at times I've been much more critical of the kinds of privileges and respect and disjunction that have been afforded to intellectuals in the European tradition, and at those times have been more appreciative of the USA's – not anti-intellectualism – but refusal of theory's claim to authority.

Q. THE WHITE REVIEW —— Have you identified with different stages in the continuum linking theory and practice at different stages in your career?

A. MICHAEL HARDT —— Yes, I suppose. It's important to recognise the autonomy of scholarship, too. It's stupid to read Spinoza only for the ways it's going to help you close down the federal building downtown. But it's exciting when you find a relationship between theory and practice. Personally as well, I felt a kind of frustration in those separated lives, with not being able to make the connection myself, but also with being in an atmosphere where you have to have two groups of friends and each one only knows one side of what you are thinking.

Q. THE WHITE REVIEW —— Your first book is on Deleuze and it's called AN APPRENTICESHIP IN PHILOSOPHY. What kind of apprenticeship was it? What was the theoretical landscape that you were entering at the time, and what was the kind of intervention you saw yourself making in it?

A. MICHAEL HARDT —— One thing is that I felt a certain need to engage with what was often posed at the time as the politics of post-structuralism, and generally the assumption that post-structuralism didn't have a politics or that the politics of deconstruction stood for those of post-structuralism as a whole. When I was writing the dissertation that then became the book, I had been in France and I felt like I was in a completely different political and cultural atmosphere. The politics seemed very clear to me, and so it seemed important to distinguish the types and uses of post-structuralism in political terms, as well as to insist that there was a certain fragment of what was lumped together as post-structuralism that seemed to me importantly political work, and not at all a flight from politics.

Q. THE WHITE REVIEW — I guess that would have been around the time that the 'End of History' arguments were making the rounds, in the early 1990s. Did you want to steer away from that type of reasoning?

A. MICHAEL HARDT — Well, there was also a very strong Anglo–American Marxist reaction against postmodernism-slash-poststructuralism, most visibly Derrida and Foucault. Deleuze and Guattari were more or less outside of that view, and yet it seemed to me both that Marxism had a lot to learn from their work and that their work could be thought of as an effort to transform and renew Marxism. It was this relationship that I was passionate about at the time.

Q. THE WHITE REVIEW — And so you wanted to learn from Deleuze's method?

A. MICHAEL HARDT — I admired his method, yes, and it came down, simply, to the way he reads. I've largely remained very dedicated to a certain kind of traditional scholarship in my career, and one thing that attracts me to Deleuze is his engagement – and then, of course, revision – within the history of philosophy. He taught me how to read other philosophers, to think through them. An apprenticeship implies to me, too, that there isn't a question of mastery or finding faults, or even positioning yourself in a stable relationship of critique to an author. What Deleuze does that frustrates many people but seemed really empowering to me at the time was that he doesn't approach Bergson or Nietzsche and say 'This is really helpful, but this is wrong', and separate out this from that idea. The stuff he disagrees with he totally ignores. Bergson's Christianity? It doesn't even appear. From a certain perspective, one could say that he's irresponsible, if one thinks that our responsibility is to evaluate authors or evaluate the tradition. Instead, he develops what he can, he makes good on what he can, makes use of what he can. That's the way that I thought of the apprenticeship, and that's what got me excited. I had a great deal of pleasure doing that project.

Q. THE WHITE REVIEW — Deleuze talks about his method as a kind of buggery, specifically in relation to Kant. He says that you have to take Kant from behind and produce a monstrous child.

A. MICHAEL HARDT — What Deleuze likes about that image, I think, is that the product is not a reproduction of Kant, not a derivation of Kant, but a new creation. That makes sense to me, but I just felt like I was trying to understand what the hell Deleuze was saying, and thought that if I tried to explain that the best that I could, it would be enough. Apprenticeship also involves modesty. I didn't feel at that time that it was my aim to go beyond Deleuze to create something different, I was just trying to understand what he was saying and to understand him in relation to the pressures of certain political desires through which I read him.

Q. THE WHITE REVIEW — Let's talk about *EMPIRE*. Was it originally conceived as the first installment of a trilogy or did it begin as a self-contained project?

A. MICHAEL HARDT — *EMPIRE* started very indirectly. A French publisher proposed to Toni Negri that he write a textbook on political philosophy, and Toni proposed to me that we work on it together. Originally, we had envisioned it as focusing on the concept of sovereignty and its historical development. Eventually, the relationship with the publisher and the textbook idea didn't work out, and so the project was free to evolve from there.

Q. THE WHITE REVIEW — But the idea of sovereignty as a cornerstone remained?

A. MICHAEL HARDT — Right, sovereignty as a way of structuring a historical account of political thought. That's how it stood in our earliest outlines. The shift to when the book was no longer strictly accountable for the history and no longer in textbook form was crucial, though, because already then we understood in some sense that the ways in which the modern tradition conceptualised sovereignty no longer applied, had shifted. It was from there that EMPIRE became the theoretical point of departure. The more banal, day-to-day point of departure was that, with the first Gulf War, we thought we were seeing something different than a familiar mode of US imperialism. There was a new kind of power structure in formation, and we thought that anti-Americanism — meaning anti-US-ism — simply wasn't an adequate ideological position. That feeling intersected with this notion of a shift in the nature of sovereignty.

Q. THE WHITE REVIEW — Other theorists argue that, within the multifaceted context of EMPIRE, instead of shrinking the State actually exerts its sovereignty more forcefully — that it proliferates laws with regard to things like intellectual property and labour rights — in reaction to its slipping grasp on power.

A. MICHAEL HARDT — It's not a matter of the State getting stronger or weaker, but rather the State getting fitted into a different context. I remember being quite frustrated in these discussions where one person would say that globalisation exists and so the State no longer matters, and the other person would say that the State still matters and therefore there is no globalisation. It's rather that state structures now fit within a much larger context to which they have to become adequate. One person who is really good about this is Saskia Sassen, who describes in great detail the processes of the denationalisation of the State. I find it quite convincing, for instance, when she analyses the changing roles of the kind of people who go to the World Economic Forum meetings in Davos. There, you have state functionaries like national economics ministers together with global corporate leaders. The ministers have to engineer state policies while simultaneously keeping the constitution of the global economic system in mind. It's not that they no longer fulfil their functions as economic ministers of Turkey and Japan but that they now act in relation to a different ultimate scene, at once national and global.

In the same way, any way of thinking the global order today has to take the power of states into account. The question is the context in which they fit. In the same way, it's not that the US no longer matters — it still matters a lot, in fact — but that it no longer has the power to dictate global affairs in the way it has in the past in Latin America and that neoconservatives imagined ten years ago that it could in the Middle East. All of this has a rather dramatic effect on the State. It's not at all the same as it once was, and in fact, taking the perspective of sovereignty is exactly what poses this newness in greatest relief.

Q. THE WHITE REVIEW — Did you know, while you were working on EMPIRE, that there were going to be two subsequent books?

A. MICHAEL HARDT — Absolutely not, no. No, we felt we were lucky to finish one!

Q. THE WHITE REVIEW — Did either of you foresee the response that the book got? Had you calculated your approach for a certain kind of reception or was it a total surprise?

A. MICHAEL HARDT — Mostly it got a lot of

attention about a year after it was published. But it did get a certain amount of attention immediately. No, we never expected much, especially mainstream, attention. I remember my partner said at the time that Toni and I had a small and highly disturbed fan club. It's true, though, that we were consciously writing — not exactly a summation — but trying to bring together different strands of autonomous Marxisms in one place. We were conscious, in that sense, of writing for those who were already interested in the tradition and of trying to pull things together.

Q. THE WHITE REVIEW —— Your goal was a kind of coalition-building, in political terms?

A. MICHAEL HARDT —— We weren't so much thinking about it in political terms as in intellectual terms. There were a variety of intellectual paradigms that seemed to us either adjacent or verging on similar ideas — post-structuralism and Marxism, as we've already said, but also post-colonial studies, socialist feminism and certain feminist theory in general, queer theory. The idea was not exactly coalition-building but trying to recognise the coincidences and relationships among a variety of theoretical paradigms, perspectives, traditions. In that sense, *EMPIRE* was a very academic project.

Q. THE WHITE REVIEW —— You mean academic in the sense that you weren't expecting a bestseller.

A. MICHAEL HARDT —— We were pretty lucid about the obstacles in the way of the book being read by more than this small and highly disturbed fan club. Firstly, yes, a very academic book; secondly, a book that calls itself communist; and then, thirdly, the deviation, even if not always announced, from the dominant Marxist tradition. On each of these counts, it certainly wasn't an operation of engineering a book that would sell a lot of copies. We were very pleased to get a contract with a major university press. Toni was particularly pleased. He thought — and I think it's true — that for his legal situation and certainly for his immediate image in Italy, having a book from Harvard University Press meant a lot, and meant more than any other university press just because of the stupid media image of Harvard in other countries. So that appealed to us.

Q. THE WHITE REVIEW —— When you finished writing *EMPIRE*, was it clear which direction you needed to take with your next work?

A. MICHAEL HARDT —— We weren't immediately thinking about writing another book. We did already have criticisms of the book in mind. On one hand, there was an intellectual agenda that arose out of it for us. I remember writing letters to each other about our dissatisfaction with the concept of the multitude as it was articulated in *EMPIRE*. Not that we thought it was wrong; we just thought it wasn't worked out. We'd first talked about multitude primarily in terms of the dominant countries and this notion of immaterial labour, but we knew then that if it was going to mean anything it would have to be equally true and relevant in the context of subordinated countries. That got me started doing research about peasantry for a while, agriculture, that sort of thing. On the other hand, we were also swept up in a really exciting political period. The Seattle WTO protests [of November 1999] happened while the book was in production. In fact, in hindsight I'm glad that I didn't, but I remember thinking at the time that I should get a picture of Seattle as the cover of the book because I felt like it was a real moment of realisation, like, 'Oh, that's what we were talking about!'

Then there were the World Social Forums, different globalisation protest movements. A lot of MULTITUDE, the book, was in dialogue with and inspired by those developments, trying to enter into dialogue, to learn from them. MULTITUDE, more than the other books, has a very specific historical context and date. It's much more embedded in a moment.

Q. THE WHITE REVIEW —— You've spoken in other interviews about the joys of political life, that there is a positive valence – not just a lack – to struggle and political desire. How do you regard your own work with regard to this dichotomy between, say, affirmation and critique? Did the critique of sovereignty in EMPIRE require a complement in MULTITUDE and later in COMMONWEALTH?

A. MICHAEL HARDT —— It's sometimes difficult to talk about critique because so many things are meant by the term, from a properly Kantian procedure to simply expressing a dissatisfaction with the way things are, even fault-finding. What's most important to me is the question of alternative. What seems insufficient to me, with regard to a certain type of politicised scholarship that has been predominant in the academy over the last twenty years, is a critical practice that does not include the proposition of alternatives, that in fact assumes that the invalidity of the form of power, or the revelation of injustice itself, will somehow lead to the creation of something new. Critiques of US foreign policy or discourses on the ideological functions of Hollywood films, at least in their garden variety forms, rely on the notion that if the people only knew, they would change. Revealing the truth about power is in this sense a critical operation. The problem is that a kind of melancholy arises within political scholarship when those incredibly well-developed and well-articulated revelations of the truth about power in fact *don't* then inspire or lead to anything else.

It's important to know the truth about the history of US interventions in Latin America, for instance, but it isn't sufficient, and that fact is increasingly obvious today in a way that maybe wasn't obvious to previous generations. There are at least two – I don't exactly think they're straw figures – but let's say two limit points we're up against. One, in which a certain stream of anarchist thought assumes the spontaneity of alternative social formation, of collaboration, of mutual aid, etc. – a stream of thought not just in favour of revealing and removing the constraints of dominating power, but against power as such. The other limit would be the form of critique in which we need the perpetual revelation of the truth about power to keep it in check. That's the theological figure: *katechon*, holding back evil.

Q. THE WHITE REVIEW —— Critique is also much easier than the proposition of alternatives.

A. MICHAEL HARDT —— Well, I think the disjunct between the two can also be thought about in terms of power. Within the world of politicised scholarship, critique is a mark of sophistication whereas actually proposing something is a position of weakness, because anyone could critique it. Or take Marcuse's position on affirmative culture. For him, affirmation meant an absence of critique, and hence is not just naïve, but actually sustains the current ruling order. One can affirm only what exists; critique, the negative movement, is necessary to create something new. That much seems absolutely right to me, but what's crucial is that the negative movement has to be accompanied by a constitutive one. Rather than a position of purity dedicated to perpetual critique we need to create or theorise or recognise the real possibilities of a social alternative.

Q. THE WHITE REVIEW — The question is where those alternatives come from. You and Toni have theorised the notion of a materialist teleology for revolution — revolution as self-regulating, or as a kind of logbook of political desire rather than an outcome-oriented strategy — as an alternative to utopian programmes that fail to generate immediate, concrete political action.

A. MICHAEL HARDT — I like the idea of a materialist teleology because I'm equally dissatisfied with the notion of teleology as an end dragging history towards it and the idea of spontaneous, unguided political formation. The goals of revolution come from political struggle itself, and I like the idea that, as you say, there is a sort of celestial logbook registering the sum total of those radical individual desires that drive historical change in a real direction, not only a *cahier de doléances*, as in pre-revolutionary France, but also a *cahier des désirs politiques, des luttes politiques*. Toni and I have become increasingly involved with formulating a theory of the institutionalisation of political desire. We struggle with that term, 'institution', because we don't mean it as some new bureaucratic structure or even a party in the traditional form; what we mean by institution is something closer to the way anthropologists talk about the repeated habits and forms that create social continuity. There is such a thing as spontaneous revolt — people do revolt against their conditions in a way that is not always orchestrated in advance — but once that act of rebellion occurs, it has to be organised, formed, institutionalised in the sense of being repeated and made into something lasting.

Q. THE WHITE REVIEW — Some of your recent work has attempted to explore the theoretical potential for the concept of love. Do you see the political concept of love, as you theorise it, as the kind of power capable of filling the gap of continuity?

A. MICHAEL HARDT — I have become interested in the idea of deriving the necessity of a political concept of love, but maybe a better way of getting at the problem at hand would be an example from when I first met Toni. As a graduate student in Seattle, I had been interested in and inspired by some things about Italy in general and Toni's work in particular. At that time, he was clandestine in France in a very ambiguous sort of way, and so in order to meet him I arranged to work on an English translation of his Spinoza book — a friend in Paris got me in touch with him by phone, and he said why don't you come to Paris, we'll talk about translation stuff. So I went there for a week, and the primary discussion we had during that week was about the problem of the lack, in English, of two separate words for power. In Latin, and so in Italian and French and other European languages, there are two different concepts — significantly different in Spinoza and so also a sensitive matter in Toni's work — both commonly translated into English as 'power'. Neither of us were satisfied with our attempts at salvaging these concepts in an English word.

Q. THE WHITE REVIEW — What kind of problems did that pose for the project?

A. MICHAEL HARDT — Well, the first, in Latin, *potestas*, is a centralised and in some sense transcendent power, in Spinoza often associated with God or the State; the other, *potentia*, is an immanent and usually plural power arising from below. In Spinoza, at least, there is a rather clear distinction. Once

I became sensitised to it, though, I started recognising that in a common French theoretical vocabulary, too – in Foucault, in Deleuze and others – this difference between *pouvoir* and *puissance* had a roughly similar valence. So why, in English, do we just have this one word, power? This has very real effects. If you think of power as a unitary concept, then the critique of power can easily become an anti-power position; whereas with two concepts of power, it can be the struggle against one and for the other, an argument for a better, different power. The distinction is helpful with regard to the possibilities for a critique of power that can simultaneously be the argument for an alternative.

Q. THE WHITE REVIEW —— Let's talk about how these ideas actually get played out in everyday political struggle. Writing in the *GUARDIAN* [24 February 2011], you recognised the need in Egypt for an alternative order that neither replaces the existing elite with a new one nor sacrifices the democratic mandate of this collective action. Where, in your opinion, do Egyptians go from here? Are there any important lessons to be learned from the recent history of Latin America?

A. MICHAEL HARDT —— It is helpful, I think, to make recourse to Latin America and the struggles that took place there over the last decade and more. Specifically for the Egypt of 2011, the Argentina of 2001 seems a useful comparison. There, it wasn't so much the overthrow of a dictator as the overthrow of the neoliberal order and the governing caste that went with it. In both cases, the forces involved were comprised of a rather wide network of political protests and demands, and in both cases, the overthrow of one political leadership was only the beginning of a long process. What was so interesting about the developments in Argentina at the time was the experimentation with new democratic forms, the construction of assembly movements in the attempt to work out a new kind of governance through delegation and discussion. Other practices, too: workers taking over the factories, the organisation and protests of the unemployed, barter systems, a whole range of efforts to construct alternative political and social forms.

In hindsight, most of the self-critique from those who were involved during those years involves the failure to create the means of continuity. They were left with something that was much better than what they started with, a new government that was indebted to and that maintained relationships with the social movements that established it, but it was not at all what they had aspired to during that time of potential. It's partly in that context that I think one can evaluate what the developments in Egypt should be after the overthrow of the tyrant. There has to be a progressive and continuous experimentation within that social transformation, and these experiments have to become institutions in the sense of habits of repeated social relation. Another way would be to think in constitutional terms, of constitutionalising new freedoms, new means of relation, new economic orders. Each of these, institution and constitution, points in a different way to solidifying the creation of alternatives.

Q. THE WHITE REVIEW —— Do you think that new technology transforms the possibilities of democracy or revolution beyond a simple acceleration of the kinds of historical cycles that were already in motion?

A. MICHAEL HARDT —— New technology isn't an answer to the question of organisation but it does provide ever more powerful mechanisms with which to construct new social forms and institutions. There are still limits. Ten years ago, when the internet came up in politics, it was common to hear people talk about inequality of access; today, with phones, that's changed a bit, but it's still important to recognise that in a country like Egypt different populations organise within different, often overlapping networks. A vast majority of the population has access to Al-Jazeera as a network; it's only a new and relatively small demographic that has a substantial relationship to Twitter.

Q. THE WHITE REVIEW — So, as Marx would have it, the conditions of possibility for realising new forms of social relation are immanent to the system, and recognising new potentials requires the conscious development of an ethics of that system.

A. MICHAEL HARDT — An ethics is one thing, but also basic structures and institutions, like, 'How are we going to decide things?' It will be interesting to learn more about how exactly decisions were made in the square in Cairo. In the Argentinean assembly movements, they were attempting, sometimes unsuccessfully, to work out new ways of structuring democracy, new methods of resolving conflicts. Technology doesn't solve that, but it does allow for new possibilities.

Q. THE WHITE REVIEW — And yet, the geography of contemporary politics seems to pose a problem. In Egypt or Wisconsin, protesters can show up at Mubarak's palace or the State Capitol building; for others, political desire is immediately confronted by several difficulties: the dispersed political geography of EMPIRE, the immaterial nature of power, the lack of traditional public domain in which to be seen. Does political activism today have a target, or is there a new organisational principle — smartmobs, hacktivism, etc. — that better engages this kind of terrain?

A. MICHAEL HARDT — One thing that has been quite well developed theoretically is the idea that locations of power are really only stand-ins for a much more generalised type of power. In some ways, the discourse on neoliberalism functioned that way — as in, it might be the IMF that's doing this, or this national government, but the real enemy is neoliberalism in whatever material form it takes. It's clear to everyone involved that Mubarak himself could not actually embody the enemy. Furthermore, from what we know of what's happened so far in Egypt and Tunisia and Libya and elsewhere, the protests have not been oriented fundamentally towards or against the US. As far as I've been able to understand it so far, these struggles have not yet developed a theory of the enemy.

This may be OK for certain groups in certain moments, but identifying the enemy is still really an important and not-trivial political task, a crucial part of the theoretical development within political activity. That's what Toni and I thought we were doing in EMPIRE, attempting to name the coming enemy — the enemy-in-formation — with the simple idea that it matters for our practices of resistance and even for our political imagination what it is that we're facing. It's not exclusively an academic question. It's politically relevant how we understand the problem: if the dominant forms of control today are different and dispersed and plural, then we have to define new ways of challenging them. It has to be a process. That's another lesson to take from the experience in Latin America: there's a kind of back and forth, a dialectic in a weak sense, between progressive governments that constantly disappoint and social movements that constantly challenge, a kind of approximating movement. It's not just a question of success or failure but an approach of some kind, a continuing movement.

Q. THE WHITE REVIEW — Another scene of some remarkable political activity over the last few months is the US prison system. You've spent some time working in prisons, organising reading groups and teaching Louis Althusser to inmates. How did that come about?

A. MICHAEL HARDT — I was mostly teaching Foucault, but it's the same sort of thing. This actually brings us all the way back to the beginning of the interview. I went through different bouts of frustration with academic politics, and this was one that started directly after I went to a conference in the early 1990s. Perhaps a bit dramatically, I went home and called the state prison system to try to find a way to work in the prisons. I had a postdoctoral position in Los Angeles at the time, and that seemed to me the most practical kind of political engagement available. So, I worked for a year in the state prison in Chino, east of Los Angeles, and the next year I worked at a jail in Bridgeport, Connecticut, and then when I came to Duke I did five years of teaching a course on justice in the federal prison in Butner.

Q. THE WHITE REVIEW — Were there any major differences trying to teach theory in a prison environment rather than in a university classroom?

A. MICHAEL HARDT — Actually, there was one time I had graduate students participate with the inmates in a joint reading of Michel Foucault's DISCIPLINE AND PUNISH. I got permission from the prison administration to have fifteen students come, and the prisoners prepared punch and cookies for our meeting, and we just sat down together and talked Foucault. We had also read Goffman's ASYLUMS and one other book in that vein, and the interesting thing was that in discussing each of those books, the Foucault in particular, the inmates were very upset about the construction of subjectivity, the way in which institutions create a subjectivity. They thought of that as political defeat. Naïve as I was, I said 'Well, actually, I think of resistance as coming from within, that we're constructed by the institutions but that from within them we can transform them'. They were not buying it, and it was really very instructive for me, very challenging. I don't bring up the example like I have any resolution to it.

Q. THE WHITE REVIEW — Let's talk a little bit more about publishing. In the last issue we spoke to André Schiffrin about the state of the industry, and this review has a stake in the question. What are your opinions on the possibilities for creative intellectual work in today's marketplace of ideas?

A. MICHAEL HARDT — I'm not sure if this is what you are asking, but it was important for me at one time, thinking back to when I was younger, to simply recognise how compromised or corrupted we all already are. I had a dissatisfaction with what seemed to be a kind of politics of purity, as if we could separate ourselves from dominant ideology and Hollywood movies and patriarchal thinking and the immaterial forces of the marketplace of ideas. We can't, but the inability to separate ourselves doesn't mean we then have to affirm it. Struggle always exists in a kind of murky landscape, but recognising how one is already compromised shouldn't be an obstacle to the attempt to do something within that context, to be a force of resistance. One can and must do it from within.

Q. THE WHITE REVIEW — Does that relate at all to your own experiences with publishing?

A. MICHAEL HARDT — Toni and I were actually very happy to publish *Empire* at what seemed to us to be — well, it's not as if Harvard University Press is reactionary in itself, it's more like it stands as a symbol of a kind of power, and the contrast with the content of the book was pleasurable to us. The other option would have been to just distribute it ourselves and avoid having any 'selling of books' whatsoever.

Q. THE WHITE REVIEW — Are you happy with the kind of impact and visibility that your writing has had? You don't object to the fact, for instance, that all of your books are easily downloadable?

A. MICHAEL HARDT — No, I'm thrilled about that. I think it's great. Here's the thing that surprised me about that whole time period surrounding the publication of *Empire*. There was a brief phase of media attention of an unusual, even weird kind around the book and around our collaboration. It went precisely from the day that the *New York Times* ran its story about the book, in the summer a full year after it came out, until 11 September [2001]. Part of it is just coincidental of course, but it was also, in hindsight, a period of curiosity, of a collective feeling that there was something new happening in the world — changes in global order, in protests and activism — that we didn't yet have a way of understanding. The book fit the moment, in that regard. Once 11 September happened, all of that completely closed down, all of the traditional narratives came back in force: political Islam, US imperialism, all of them. It's only now, ten years later, slowly, that there is re-emerging again a broader feeling of the need to rethink the current global system and global order. It's exciting.

CHRISTOPHER CATANESE & KARIM WISSA
APRIL 2011

RELIGION AND THE MOVIES

BY

AIDAN COTTRELL BOYCE

WHEN THE ROMAN EMPIRE RULED THE WORLD, you could make it work for you. The women, the hospitality. You will have heard the cliché about wives in every port. You could make that happen, I promise you.

Not so much now. It's important for a man to settle down. As important as going out and being a beast and hunting is settling down.

When I came home drunk last week I dropped the baby on its head. One minute the baby was in my arms. Its face was squashed against the shiny brass of my breastplate. The next minute it toppled backwards and fell out of my arms. The bang of the baby on the floor woke my wife up. The baby's eyes opened. It didn't make a sound. It looked straight up at me. The silence was odd. My wife sat bolt upright in bed. She pointed at the baby:

'That's even more dangerous!' she said.

I knew exactly what she meant.

We ran through the streets to the hospital. I held the broken-headed baby aloft as we ran. My wife ran two paces behind us all the way. We ran all the way to the hospital in that formation.

The wages of war are not enough for my father-in-law. He has begun talking about opening a little Italian restaurant. He claims that it is something he has always dreamed of, but I find this hard to believe. When I was a little boy, there were pictures of my father-in-law in our history textbooks. The pictures showed him drinking from a goblet full of blood. His jaw jutted out and the blood ran in little streams from the sides of his mouth. Now he wants to open a little Italian restaurant.

The reason for the restaurant is that he wants something to leave to my wife and my baby when he passes on. It's partly a nice thought, and it's partly a nice fuck you to myself.

The nurse talked to us in a patronising way. She told us that the doctor was going to open up the baby's head to make sure that nothing went wrong when it had the fall. She said 'the fall' to mean something specific. It meant: I know it was you asshole. I told the nurse that I was perfectly aware of the procedure. My wife punched me in the back. She says that I sound stupid when I use big words. It sounds (she says) like I don't know what they mean.

We watched the operation through a window. Behind the glass was a huge trestle table. On the table sat six babies. Each one of the babies was being worked on by a doctor. Some of them had holes in the backs of their heads. Some of them had had the whole top of their skull removed. The sight was horrendous in the extreme, but you've got to watch, because it's your child in there. It's the least you can do. The doctors looked relaxed anyway. They had pencils stuck behind their ears. A couple of them were smoking.

There was a time when I wanted to quit the Romans. This was before I settled down and when I was tired of the constant moving around. The law was that you could get out of the Romans as long as you had another job secured. People would take days off specifically to go to job interviews. I went to one interview, which I remember went very badly. In the Romans, your hobbies are supposed to be sports. Out of the Romans, it's not the same. When they asked me what my hobbies were in the interview, I replied that I liked sports. The interview panellists looked at me as if I'd cursed.

'We're not interested in that here,' one of them said.

There was an awkward silence before they asked if there was anything else. They looked put-out.

'I like movies.' I said. The expressions didn't change.

'Anything else?'

'I like religion.' I said.

The toilets at the hospital stank. I gagged when I walked in. Standing at the single urinal, I realised that there was a man in the cubicle taking a shit. You could hear it. It was disgusting. It was all I could think about while I was standing there, with my penis out at the urinal.

'What kind of an animal,' I kept thinking. 'At a hospital of all places.'

When the shitting man came out of the cubicle, I saw that he had long hair, and wore jeans and a denim shirt. I glared at him as I dried my hands under the electric drier. He looked back at me as if I were a psychotic. He looked as if he didn't know what he had done.

There were two new people in the baby-surgery waiting-room. My wife was standing up to the glass but the other two women were sitting on chairs by a coffee table. One was reading a magazine while the second rocked back and forth, weeping quietly. I tried to decide which approach was best, which camp we should align ourselves with. When I went up to stand by my wife, I could see that her eyes were closed. She was very beautiful, even more beautiful when she looked in danger like this. She felt my presence next to her, and turned, and opened her eyes. She looked at me.

'You'll tell him of course. Since it was your fault,' she said.

I told her about the scumbag in the men's room, and did an impression of his haircut.

'You'll tell him,' she said again.

My relationship with my father-in-law is complicated. That the man does not like me is plain to see. I'm not sure what his dislike stems from. Perhaps I am not the natural Roman that he was, but I've worked at it harder than he has. It's more difficult to become a Roman than it is to be born one. He came from a time and a place when it was like: 'Sure! Be a Roman! What the fuck else?' I was born a long time after he was.

Over many years now, a thin gestural friendliness has characterised our relationship. I don't really have a choice. My father-in-law dotes on my wife, and vice versa. My father-in-law dotes on the baby, and vice versa. I have this dream sometimes. In the dream, I am Rapunzel, high in the tower, waiting for a prince to rescue me. When the prince finally arrives, he turns out to be my father-in-law. He lights fires in a circle, all around the base of the tower. His facial expression doesn't change all the way through the dream. When I start to smell the smoke, I realise the impossibility of it all and I wake up.

When the baby was finished with its operation, it was taken to the hospital nursery. The patronising nurse told us that it would be ready for us to collect in the morning. I asked a reasonable question about the shape of its head. The nurse smiled:

'Its head is back to normal, sir.'

'Have you actually seen the baby?' I asked.

The nurse smiled. My wife punched me in the back.

When I was younger my father would collect me on weekends and take me back to his place. It was above a pub. He was a bad parent. He would pass me around all the deadbeats and slappers in the pub. Everybody would say what a handsome boy I was. I'm still not sure how that works. Is that what people say about all baby boys? Whenever I ask people that question, they think that I'm making a point.

When we left the hospital, I took my wife to the pier to cheer her up. At the entrance to the pier we bought candyfloss. My wife likes the way she can open her mouth as wide as she can and as soon as the candyfloss meets her saliva, it dwindles away to nearly nothing. All along the pier, she gulped her candyfloss and giggled as she felt it disappearing inside her. When she was done with hers, she had mine.

I know that my wife sleeps with her father's friends. I know that she is embarrassed to be seen with me in public. I know that she wishes she could wear high-heeled shoes without being taller than me. I know that she loves our baby more than she loves me. I know that I am no longer part of her family.

We stood at the end of the pier. She slipped her hand into mine and began writing things with her index finger onto my palm. I lost track of what she was writing. A man in jeans sidled up to me and my wife and offered us a bagful of cannabis. I turned and glared at him. I rapped on my breastplate.

'Do you know what this means, son?' I screeched.

'Is it a gay thing?' he asked.

Last night, for the second time in a week, I disturbed my wife and my baby in the night. I was woken up by a strange scratching sound and became aware that there was a bird in my bedroom. I knew how dangerous birds were for babies. I wasn't going to have my baby's eyes pecked out by a pigeon, or my wife's eyes for that matter.

The windows were open. The wind blew the curtains out, horizontal, into the room. The bird darted about. It perched on a cabinet, then on the chest of drawers, then on the baby's crib. I clutched a newspaper, and lurched towards it, the duvet caught between my legs. I swung at the bird and knocked my wife's jewellery box clattering to the floor. Diamonds and rubies rattled across the stone. The noise woke my wife. She saw the bird, perched above her baby's head.

'Get him out of here!' she bellowed.

'I'm trying, I'm trying!' I yelped.

'Get it out of here!' she howled.

'I'm trying!' I squeaked.

The bird crowed and cackled, and tangled itself in the billowing curtains. The sound of my high-pitched squeaking made my wife laugh. She laughed and laughed, as I clattered around the room chasing the terrified bird. The baby was awake by now, and hearing his mother's tinkling laugh, he began to giggle himself. Even though it was after midnight, the phone began to ring.

THREE POETS
AND THE WORLD

BY

CALEB KLACES

IN 1925, AGED 20, THE HUNGARIAN POET ATTILA JÓZSEF WAS EXPELLED from the University of Szeged for a radical poem published in a periodical. He left Hungary for Vienna, where he squatted in a slum with tens of thousands of other people, many of them refugees from Eastern Europe. He sold newspapers outside restaurants and cleaned university buildings. As he did for much of his life, he lived in housing he had no formal right to, and earned a living without a wage, unrecognised by the state. He existed, to use a modern phrase, in the informal economy.

After four months in 'that frightful slum', József had a rare stroke of luck. He was invited by the Hatvany family to live at their mansion. Even for those without benefactors with mansions to share, over the next few decades more and more Viennese residents became, as it were, legitimate (give or take a Nazi invasion). Land rights were formalised, social housing was built and slums diminished, as they did across Western and Northern Europe.

It seems unlikely that the informal settlements of the global south will dwindle as did their forebears in Europe, at least in the near future. In fact, slums are getting bigger. According to the UN's 2003 report 'The Challenge of Slums', in 2001 around 924 million people, or 32 per cent of the world's total urban population, lived in slums. In the first thirty years of this millennium that number is likely to double. The term 'slum' is usually defined by standard of living rather than rights to land, although it is often used interchangeably with 'informal' or 'extra-legal settlement'. In developing countries, the majority of people living in slums are also employed in the informal economy.

Contemporary slums are in many ways similar in the conditions they provide for their residents to those of Vienna in the 1920s or Manchester in the 1850s. Most lack basic amenities, are cramped, crowded and susceptible to the rapid spread both of diseases and flames. But whereas Victorian slums were largely a product of the industrial revolution, in the last few decades there has been, as Mike Davis puts it in *PLANET OF SLUMS*, mass 'urbanisation without industrialisation'. The growth of huge informal settlements on the fringes of cities, in some cases larger than the cities themselves, has not necessarily followed economic growth. Davis argues that many poorer countries have been hamstrung by the 'anti-rural' terms of loans given to them for economic development by the World Bank and IMF, by which privatisation and the loss of a public sector safety net has been encouraged or even necessitated. Millions of people have moved from rural poverty in the hope of unpoor urban living, and instead ended up living in informal developments, subdividing the limited work available with those who were already urban.

The experiences of people living outside of the formal structures, their measures of deprivation and happiness, are of course diverse. But they share with József the condition of having 'no country'. The speaker of 'With a Pure Heart', the poem that ended József's academic career at the university, is a stateless orphan with no lover now and no grave when he is dead. He is a person without rights to being a person in an area where political representation is suspended, where normal rules don't apply. From no man's land, being no one, the poem's way of asserting a self is radical and still shocking. 'With a pure heart, I'll burn and loot. | If I have to, I'll even shoot'; he will die fighting and earn a burial, so that 'death-bringing grass will start | growing from my beautiful, pure heart'. If being is being able to make things happen (as he wrote later in 'Night in the Slums': 'damp and clinging wind | is nothing | but a fluttering of dirty bed sheets', *tr.* Bakti) then his only way to be is to allow seeds to take root in his body. This is his abject redemption.

Should Western nations be cautious of a supranational class of people who bear against them legitimate complaints? Davis thinks so: '[i]f the point of the war on terrorism is to pursue the enemy into his sociological and cultural labyrinth, then the poor peripheries of developing cities will be the permanent battlefields of the twenty-first century' (IN PRAISE OF BARBARIANS). His use of the term 'war on terrorism' sounds dated, but the question Davis implies, of what sort of battlefield the poor peripheries of cities might be, is a good one. What might resistance look like? What ideas or practices might be resisted and in whose terms?

In 1927, two years after 'With a Pure Heart', József wrote a letter to his sister, in which he described the 'two fronts' of the world, 'imperialism and bolshevism': England and Russia, capitalism and communism. He felt forced to align himself with one side or the other. But by early 1933 he had been ejected from the Communist Party for what it called his 'Fascism'. Despite having sided, in his spiritedly scrutinising and peculiar way, with Russia, he was again in that familiar place, out on his own.

In his later poems, the 'I' expands to include a cast of characters. The question of how to have any agency at all gives way to other, broader questions, such as how to imagine a society that respects and celebrates technology, the modern cosmopolitan city, the 'fragile villages', and each person's freedom. The world was not short of supposed solutions and one can feel the great effort in József's poems to resist, to remain in an unconscripted place. This he frequently identifies as the city's edge, the outskirts, places that are neither one thing nor the other, makeshift settlements, slums. 'Set fire to heaven's domains' he commands in 'On the Edge of the City', a vivid rejection of utopia. The poem lets heaven burn

> [t]ill it lights up our lovely sense of order,
> that urge to shapeliness
> by which the brain knows and acknowledges
> finite unboundedness:

> the outward forces of production and the inward
> instinctive drive to bliss...
>> (*tr.* Ozsváth and Turner)

The paradox of 'finite unboundedness' could be the imagination, or spirit, in the limits of the body. There is also the relationship, here expressed in terms remarkably similar to Freud's theories of libido and the death drive, between those forces and a society that must suppress and sublimate them for the good of the whole, leaving citizens discontent but alive (CIVILISATION AND ITS DISCONTENTS had been published in Germany two years before, although I do not know if József had read it). The poem sets above these terms the 'urge to shapeliness', an impulse to acknowledge as unavoidable the paradoxes and compromises of communal living without resorting to brutality. And it is the 'city's edge' that 'sirens this wordless song'. Wordless because it is not a programme but an expression simply of resistance and hope.

This stands in contrast to the atmosphere of 'Night in the Slums'. Here is potential movement but no movement. Here is the augur of change but no change. Everything is static. A 'lonely workman [...] drinks to the revolution', while the 'wind, stray dog, wanders around'. Looking beyond, out on the 'barren fields', there is a 'scrap | of paper. How it wants to move! | It stirs, but has no strength to leave' (Bákti). József was well aware both of the necessity for the 'mumbling worker' to strive towards an altered system and the dangers of revolutions gone wrong. The result is an emphatic unmoving.

Davis sees resistance from the contemporary global underclass as coming in the form of terrorist 'chaos' rather than proletarian revolution, József's 'burn and loot'. To the other, more mysterious and hopeful 'urge to shapeliness' might be contrasted W. G. Sebald's resignation that

> the revolutions of great
> systems cannot be righted,
> too diffuse are
> the workings of power.

Sebald's book-length poem AFTER NATURE follows the wide arcs of great systems through what they have concealed or destroyed. That is, where József went to the city's edge to find a place to be wordless in the noise of the present, Sebald wandered there, as he did later in THE RINGS OF SATURN and AUSTERLITZ, in part to give words to some silenced past.

'Dark Night Sallies Forth', the third and final section of AFTER NATURE, begins with what seems to be a gloss on how to read the rest. The narrative leaps from

Sebald's grandparents' marriage (in the year József was born, incidentally) to a class photograph of the couple's children in 1917, and on again to another photograph of Sebald's parents taken on 26 August 1943. The next day, Sebald's father left for Dresden, and here Sebald himself enters the narrative through a question later put to his father, who cannot, no, remember the beauty of that city. The next day, 582 aircraft destroyed Nuremberg and his mother realised she was pregnant.

It is only later, when he views a painting of Lot and his daughters with 'a terrible conflagration' blazing behind them, that Sebald can see for the first time what his parents cannot or will not remember. (In a series of lectures collected as ON THE NATURAL HISTORY OF DESTRUCTION, Sebald wondered at length why Germans have not been able to recognise and mourn for the destruction of their cities by the Allies.) He has seen it all before. It is Nuremberg and Dresden. His father's lie comes closest to the senseless truth, and 'a little later, | crossing to Floridsdorf | on the Bridge of Peace, | I nearly went out of my mind'.

The poem returns to the edges again and again. Sebald was born 'on the northern | edge of the Alps' on an inauspicious day in 1944, when someone in the village was killed in a storm. Despite this coincident catastrophe he grew up 'without any | idea of destruction'. His move to Manchester in 1966, where he 'took lodgings | among the previous century's | ruins', can be understood at least in part as a self-imposed exile, an effort to find the destruction that had always seemed to happen beyond his apprehension at home.

> In his excitement about the truly
> boundless growth
> of industry, the statesman
> Disraeli called Manchester
> the most wonderful city of modern times,
> a celestial Jerusalem
> whose significance only philosophy
> could gauge.

I wonder about the image in Disraeli's mouth. The statesman's famous remark about Manchester, through a character in his 1844 novel CONNINGSBY, is that it was 'as great a human exploit as Athens'. Sebald's alteration is slight, but significant. There is great hubris in either pronouncement, but if Sebald is misreading Disraeli, Disraeli misreading the city, where does that place us in relationship to what we read—whether it is a poem like this, or the city it describes? The emphatic 'truly' serves ironically, too, to dull the passage's ring of truth.

AFTER NATURE makes the outskirts of 1960s Manchester seem much like József's

1930s Budapest. So much is dead, disappeared or defunct. One day, searching for the 'star-shaped Strangeways | Prison', he finds himself 'in a sort of no-man's-land | behind the railway buildings'. Here, where there are vacant shops with Jewish-German names on them, Sebald finds hostels, a music hall and church; 'an old people's home, | a prison [...] an asylum'. But Manchester is oddly without the fervent, if disempowered, workers of József's later poems. There is something particularly lonely about the age AFTER NATURE sets itself as being in, 'measured by the ticking | of Geigers in the power station'. Where have all the workers gone? Nowhere to be seen and therefore present are the 'obscure crowds | who fuelled the progress of history'. Sebald imagines the breath 'of legions of human beings' trapped in rivers that then 'carried them downstream [...] out | to the sea', adding that '[t]hose silent mutations | clear the way to the future'.

It is a devastating movement, people disappearing into the vast impersonal blankness of the sea. But it is critically local, too. Despite the Irk and the Irwell being long dead, Sebald still stood on their banks. When Friedrich Engels, a contemporary of Disraeli, went on his own walks through Manchester the Irk was a 'narrow, coal-stinking river full of filth' (THE CONDITION OF THE WORKING CLASS IN ENGLAND IN 1844). Engels reported on the tightly-packed, airless houses with shared streets 'so dirty that the inhabitants can pass into and out of the court only by passing through foul pools of stagnant urine and excrement'. The dirt, waste and stink that Engels and others exposed in the slums of industrial cities has in the West now been diverted to sewers underneath, and landfill outside, the city. A largely invisible infrastructure channels unwanted and unhealthy detritus elsewhere. Sebald looks out onto the

> haunted [...] rubbish dumps
> of the City Corporation, a smouldering
> alpine range, which, it seemed to me,
> extended into the beyond.
> In the dusk I often saw
> the searchlight beams from
> bulldozers creeping about there
> that pierced the void, and aeroplanes,
> our grey primeval brothers,
> rose with infinite slowness
> from the lagoon and the bogs.

Sebald's rubbish dump seems at first read to bear no relation to the one in American poet AR Ammons' GARBAGE (1993), also a book-length poem. Ammons' tone, a rare mixture of folksy southern wryness and Latinate scientific precision (he trained as a biologist), is in a different key to Sebald's melancholy. But landfills in the north of England and in Florida are not so different. Late capitalism does not respect borders. (That said, the rubbish in Chinese landfill is more likely to be heterogeneous than in English or American. Rubbish tends to go in the cheapest rather than the nearest hole.) Ammons' poem, which is more of a long digression from *garbage* than a sustained observation of it, is also populated by the 'yellowjackets' who shift and lift and take their hats off to contemplate the rubbish. But they are not so spectral here, amongst the insects and birds that feed on the mound they make, and 'Archie', the poet, getting old and wondering what to do with himself.

Drawn as he was to the beauty of coincidence, Sebald would, I think, have appreciated the fact that almost the same number of people now live in slums as were alive when Engels first visited the streets of Manchester. Even those who do not live in a so-called '*garbage* slum' on top of a landfill site, such as Quarantina outside Beirut or Hillat Kusha outside Khartoum, live in places not too dissimilar from Ammons' landfill. As the UN says, 'slums are often recipients of the city's nuisances, including industrial effluent and noxious waste, and the only land accessible to slum dwellers is often fragile, dangerous or polluted — land that no one else wants'. With that is likely to come, in Davis' typically thumping phrase, 'excremental and existential continuities' of the kind that Ammons implicitly understands. He writes about garbage because it is also a way of writing about death. He is getting old. His colleagues are getting cancer. In the poem, he attends a funeral. He asks 'but what about the spirit, does it die | in an instant, being nothing in an instant out of matter'. He asks, 'when does a fact end: || what does one do with this gap from just yesterday | or just this morning to fifty-five billion | years — to infinity[?]'. One answer is to fill it with garbage. That is, make a stay against the eternal by making and buying stuff and sending it out beyond the city limits. Only now the mounds are starting to get in the way and the toxins are gaining a spiritual quality.

GARBAGE is a meditation on excess. Not only in the pejorative sense, which complains of the excesses of materialism, that we buy much, much more than we *need* (Ammons occasionally does think like this, but more often about what need means, when applied to various creatures including us), but also of withins and withouts, products and by-products, lives and legacies. To paraphrase Adam Phillips writing on dreams: to pay attention to garbage is to pay attention to what we make when we are not concentrating on making. It contains the waste product of the fulfilment, or partial fulfilment, of our desires. Here are the leftovers of a meeting of our 'instinctive drive to bliss' and 'the outward forces of production'. The vestiges of eating, drinking, buying and being entertained are here (in the sense that a remembered dream can sometimes be, as Phillips points out, something redundant which survives). The redundant is stubborn. But Ammons always strives to put things in a cosmic perspective, to understand waste as always on its way to being something else. The dump, like József's Heaven and Sebald's Sodom (and, some historians argue, the ancient rubbish dump outside the real Jerusalem, the sight of which led holy writers to depict hell as hot rather than its historical icy cold) is always spectacularly bursting into flames. It is at 'the burning edge of beginning and | ending' — not of ideologies or human history but of rude matter.

> Transmutation has some limits, however:
> [...] nothing
>
> much can become of the clear-through plastic
> lid: it finds hidden security in the legit
>
> museums of our desecrations — the mounds,
> the heights of discard: meaningless is the
>
> providence [... .]

'The mounds, | the heights of discard' are grand-sounding structures built out of the giving up of opportunities ('discard' was originally de-card, to throw away a card from the hand). They are measures of not doing.

Davis argues that what he calls the fastest-growing class of people on earth doesn't fit into 'the current neoliberal regime of globalisation'. Provocatively, he refers to its members as 'a surplus humanity'. In his view, in global economic terms they are also a measure of not doing. They stand outside the flow of capital and are in some sense its product — what the rich world makes when it is not concentrating on making much but money. Can the status of the informal class be differentiated from the otiose clear-through plastic lid? Ammons' 'legit', like Sebald's 'truly', is darkly ironic.

E

[A note on translations:

I have jumped about a little between two translations of József's work. This is primarily because there is no English version of the complete József, secondarily because I prefer some versions to others. The two I quote from are quite different in tone and idiom. One is American English (John Bákti, Carcanet) and one British (Zsuzsanna Ozsváth and Frederick Turner, Bloodaxe); the former in the free spirit of Ezra Pound, the latter an attempt to get at the precise rhythms, rhyme and other formal elements of the verse in Hungarian. I have indicated which version is being used each time, and have, for clarity, stuck to the same version of a particular poem whenever it is mentioned.]

APPENDIX

PLATES

I. Portrait of William Boyd, courtesy William Boyd.
II. *Bridge No.122* from *Nat Tate: An American Artist 1928-1960* (Bloomsbury, 2011), courtesy William Boyd.
III. *Bridge No.55* from *Nat Tate: An American Artist 1928-1960* (Bloomsbury, 2011), courtesy William Boyd.
IV. *Coded and Loaded II & III* © Muhanned Cader.
V. 1989 cover of Pierre Reverdy's *Main d'œuvre, Poèmes 1913-1949*, courtesy Mercure de France.
VI–XXI. Untitled taken from the *From Back Home* series © JH Engström.
XXII. *Hart Crane* by David Alfaro Siqueiros, 1931 © DACS 2011.
XXIII. *Zenit-E* © Noam Toran and Onkar Kular.
XXIV. *7 Inch* © Noam Toran and Onkar Kular.
XXV. *Toffee Hammer* © Noam Toran and Onkar Kular.
XXVI. *Trout* © Noam Toran and Onkar Kular.
XXVII. *Farm* © Noam Toran and Onkar Kular.
XXVIII. *Revox A700* © Noam Toran and Onkar Kular.
XXIX. *Bar Mitzvah Cake* © Noam Toran and Onkar Kular.
XXX. *Longshoreman's Hooks* © Noam Toran and Onkar Kular.
XXXI. *Dentures* © Noam Toran and Onkar Kular.
XXXII. Portrait of Michael Hardt, courtesy Michael Hardt.

CONTRIBUTORS

JOSEPHINE BREESE is a London-based curator and writer. She is the director of art dealership HRL Contemporary and co-curated 'Contemporary Art from Sri Lanka' at Asia House in March 2011.

KIT BUCHAN is a poet, trumpeter and film critic. He lives in Paris, where he works as a freelance journalist. He is currently co-writing a musical and working on his first collection of poems.

CHRIS CATANESE is a writer, editor and student living in Durham, North Carolina.

JOSHUA COHEN was born in Brooklyn in 1980. He is the author, most recently, of the novel *WITZ* (Dalkey Archive Press). A collection of novellas appears next year from Graywolf Press.

AIDAN COTTRELL BOYCE was born in Liverpool in 1987. He studied theology at Bristol University and now teaches religious studies in Brighton.

SOPHIE VON CUNDALE was born in 1987. She is an artist working with video, performance and collage. She recently exhibited at Sketch, London, and her film *THE GARDEN OF ENDEMOL* will be screened at the Notting Hill Gate Theatre later this year as part of the Serpentine Gallery's Cinema Programme.

JH ENGSTRÖM was born in 1969 in the Värmland region of Sweden. Published books include *TRYING TO DANCE* (shortlisted for the Deutsche Börse Photography Prize 2005), *CDG/JHE* and *FROM BACK HOME* (with Anders Petersen). He is represented by Galerie VU, Paris, and GUN Gallery, Stockholm.

LAUREN ELKIN is a Paris-based writer and literary critic. She recently obtained her PhD in English literature, and her first novel, *FLOATING CITIES*, will be published in the fall by Editions Héloïse d'Ormesson. She teaches at New York University in France.

GRAHAM FOUST is the author of four collections of poetry. He lives and works at Saint Mary's College of California. With Samuel Frederick, he is currently translating the last two books of the late German poet Ernst Meister.

SAM GORDON is a freelance translator working from French and Spanish. He is originally from Aberdeenshire but is currently living in London.

CONTRIBUTORS

JANET HENDRICKSON's translation of *The Future Is Not Ours* (ed. Diego Trelles Paz), an anthology of short stories by young Latin American writers, will be published by Open Letter Books in 2012. Her translations have appeared in *Granta*, *Zoetrope: All-Story*, n+1 and elsewhere.

ANNABEL HOWARD's short stories and essays have appeared in magazines in the UK, Ireland and Italy. She is currently working on a non-fiction book on the subject of Italian festivals.

LEWIS IRVINE is a recent philosophy graduate based in Glasgow. He is enrolled to begin a Masters in Book Conservation. His writing has been published in various literary magazines and he is a qualified bookbinder. He is currently working on the books of several Glasgow artists.

KEITH R. JONES lives and works in Boston. He is currently working on a study of the historical imagination within contemporary American genre fiction and a collection of prose poems.

CALEB KLACES is a freelance writer, editor and poet from Birmingham. His poetry and essays have appeared or are forthcoming in *Poetry*, *Poetry London*, *The Threepenny Review* and *Rain Taxi*. A pamphlet of his poems, *All Safe All Well*, was published by Flarestack in 2011.

ONKAR KULAR's work centres around the use of design as a medium to engage with social, cultural and popular issues. His work has been exhibited internationally in London, Tokyo, Jerusalem, Rotterdam and Barnsley.

EUGENIA LAPTEVA was born and raised in Stockholm. She is currently completing her MA in Comparative Literature and Literary Theory at Goldsmith's College, London. She has written for several publications including *Sang Bleu* and *Elle*.

PATRICK MCGUINNESS teaches French at St Anne's College, Oxford. His most recent book of poems, *Jilted City*, appeared in 2010, and his novel *The Last Hundred Days*, about the end of the Ceaușescu regime in Romania, appears this year.

LEE ROURKE is the author of the short story collection *Everyday* and the novel *The Canal* (winner of the *Guardian*'s Not The Booker Prize 2010). Non-fiction work *A Brief History of Fables: From Aesop to Flash Fiction* is forthcoming in September 2011.

CONTRIBUTORS

TRISTAN SUMMERSCALE is co-editor of *Notes from the Underground*, a literary magazine and production company (www.notesfromtheunderground.co.uk). Their latest project is 'Photo Stories', an experiment in writing and photography.

NOAM TORAN was born in 1975 in Las Cruces, New Mexico. His work spans multiple disciplines and mediums, primarily involving the creation of objects and films that reflect upon the intersection between cinema, mass culture and psychology.

DIEGO TRELLES PAZ was born in Lima in 1977. He is the author of the short story collection *Hudson, el redactor* and the novel *El círculo de los escritores asesinos*. He is a professor at The State University of New York and the editor of *El futuro no es nuestro*, an anthology of short stories by young Latin American writers.

THIRZA WAKEFIELD is a freelance journalist, film critic and actress living in Paris.

AHREN WARNER was born in 1986. He has published a pocket-book, *Re:*, with Donut Press. His first full collection, *Confer*, will be published by Bloodaxe in September 2011.

RICHARD WENTWORTH was born in 1947 in Samoa. In 2002 he was made Master of the Ruskin School of Drawing and Fine Art at Oxford University. In 2005 Tate Liverpool devoted a retrospective to his work. He is currently Professor of Sculpture at the Royal College of Art.

KARIM WISSA is a Ph.D. student of literature at Duke University, working in the tradition of continental philosophy.

FRIENDS OF THE WHITE REVIEW

SALLY BAILEY
PIERS BARCLAY
ROSE BARCLAY
DAVID BARNETT
VALERIE BONNARDEL
SAM BROWN
ED BROWNE
MATHILDE CABANAS
THIBAULT CABANAS
KIERAN CLANCY
LEON DISCHE BECKER
CLAIRE DE DIVONNE
PHILIBERT DE DIVONNE
DAVID & BERNADETTE EASTHAM
MAX FARRAR
STEVE FLETCHER
HATTIE FOSTER
AUDE FOURGOUS
NATHAN FRANCIS
CYRILLE GONZALVES
MICHAEL GREENWOLD
ALEX GREINER
LEE JORDAN
JADE KOCH
LUISA DE LANCASTRE
CAROLYN LEK
CHARLES LUTYENS
EMILY LUTYENS
ALEX MCDONALD
RUPERT MARTIN
SALLY MERCER
MERCURE DE FRANCE
CYNTHIA & WILLIAM MORRISON-BELL
VANESSA NICHOLAS
VITA PEACOCK
BEN POLLNER
JORDAN RAZAVI
EDDIE REDMAYNE
GHISLAIN DE RINCQUESEN

NICOLE SIBELET
SAMUEL NOAH SOLNICK
HENRIETTA SPIEGELBERG
ANASTASIA SVOBODA
GEORGETTE TESTARD
MARILOU TESTARD
PIERRE TESTARD
VERONIQUE TESTARD
MICHAEL TROUGHTON
WEFUND.CO.UK
SIMON WILLIAMS
JOHN WITNEY
JULES WRIGHT